It's Personal: Five Questions You Should Answer to Give Every Kid Hope
Published by Orange, a division of The reThink Group, Inc.

5870 Charlotte Lane, Suite 300
Cumming, GA 30040 U.S.A.

The Orange logo is a registered trademark of The reThink Group, Inc.

Other Orange products are available online and direct from the publisher.
Visit our website at www.ThinkOrange.com for more resources like these.

ISBN: 978-1-63570-092-3

©2019 The reThink Group, Inc.

Authors: Reggie Joiner, Virginia Ward, and Kristen Ivy
Lead Editor: Mike Jeffries
Editing Team: Afton Phillips, Lauren Terrell
Design: Ryan Boon, FiveStone
Project Manager: Nate Brandt

Printed in the United States of America

First Edition 2019

3 4 5 6 7 8 9 10 11 12

05/08/19

Copies of this book are available for distribution in churches, schools, and other venues at a significant quantity discount. For more details, go to www.OrangeStore.org.

IT'S

FIVE QUESTIONS YOU SHOULD ANSWER TO GIVE EVERY KID HOPE

PERSONAL

"Love recognizes no barriers.

It jumps hurdles, leaps fences,

penetrates walls to arrive "

at its destination full of hope."

MAYA ANGELOU

IT'S PERSONAL

TABLE OF CONTENTS

CHAPTER 1

STOP BEING
SO SHALLOW

C hances are if you're reading this book, someone has asked you to become intentional about investing in the life of a few kids or teenagers. If someone else hasn't asked you yet, well, then we're asking you now.

You have officially been invited to invite yourself into someone's personal life.

Have you ever wondered how that works?

"Hello, my name is Jon. I volunteer here, so now let's start having deep, meaningful conversations." That's a little creepy. Maybe instead it just starts with remembering a name . . .and it ends with them moving into your living room. Don't worry, that almost never happens.

A few years ago, we set out to inspire leaders to get more personal in the way they approach the discipleship of the next generation.

We spent a year interviewing volunteers and discovering the pitfalls and best practices for those who work with kids and teenagers. The result of that project was a book called *Lead Small* where we outline the five roles of what we call a small group leader. A *small group leader* is anyone who shows up consistently in the lives of a few kids or teenagers to:

1. **BE PRESENT**
2. **CREATE A SAFE PLACE**
3. **PARTNER WITH PARENTS**
4. **MAKE IT PERSONAL**
5. **MOVE THEM OUT**

These five roles are still the heart of what we believe it looks like to help a young person develop authentic faith. The overwhelmingly positive response to *Lead Small* is evidence that more and more leaders have a desire to approach ministry in a way that's relational. But the five roles of a small group leader are like any list. They make a few implied assumptions. If you want to show up for kids and teenagers in a way that matters, there's at least one additional life skill you may need to figure out. Like, how to pack your own overnight bag for a retreat. Well, that and how to be personal.

In fact, we're going to get *really* personal for a minute. It's possible to lead a small group and still miss the entire point. In every profession that involves working with kids and teenagers, you will find books, speeches, lectures, and articles on how fulfilling that profession can be. We often recruit volunteers by making emotional promises. We guarantee that showing up consistently for kids and teenagers will awaken you to experience life more fully. You will suddenly feel content and purposeful. Your life will have meaning.

You will probably
laugh more,
feel more,
love more,
and wake up most mornings feeling like a hero.

Part of that is true or at least possible. But you might also wake up some mornings frustrated you have more events on your calendar, emails in your inbox, and distractions to your week. We know because we've actually done it. When this happens, leading kids starts to feel a little like one more responsibility for you to juggle. You might even find yourself thinking, "You guys know I'm not getting paid to do this, right?"

The ideas in this book are about the difference between being a fulfilled leader or a frustrated volunteer. Actually, the ideas in this book may be the essence of what it means to live a courageous, meaningful, and fulfilling life in any arena. But before we get carried away, let's talk about an approach many of us have when it comes to life and relationships.

Somewhere around middle school, most people begin to develop some coping mechanisms for dealing with rejection and disappointment. If you're honest, you have probably learned how to discern what is expected of you in certain environments and developed some image management skills. Many of us encounter hurt or grief, and we practice new defensive strategies of our own invention.

It's as if we drift into an unspoken philosophy of living. There's no author of this philosophy, yet millions of people follow the path. For now, let's call it The Shallow Way.

NOW HEAR US OUT.
SHALLOW HAS SOME INCREDIBLE BENEFITS.

A little bit of shallow allows you to smile politely, make small talk, and carry on with your day. It's the only way you can manage to spill hot coffee on your lap when you almost wreck the car because you were shouting at a family member, and then walk into work to make that presentation you rehearsed. Sometimes shallow is necessary.

Shallow might also be the reason you throw a little filter on that photo before you post it. Or the reason you move aside the pile of dirty laundry so it's out of frame. And you know what? It made for a good-looking photo. It's okay to enjoy a shallow version of people, including ourselves. Sometimes shallow is nice.

Over time, though, you can become a little too good at living a shallow life. You begin to act as if very little is worth your time. You convince yourself, "I wouldn't be able to 'fix it,' so why try?" You have a hard time caring about things you know you ought to care about. You choose comfort over risk, and certainty over curiosity.

SHALLOW IN SMALL AMOUNTS CAN PROVIDE RELIEF. BUT SHALLOW ALL THE TIME CAN LEAVE US EMPTY.

SHALLOW IN SOME RELATIONSHIPS JUST MAKES US POLITE. BUT SHALLOW IN EVERY RELATIONSHIP CAN MAKE US LONELY.

It's okay to be shallow. It's just not okay to always be shallow. Most of us know that if we live too shallow for too long, we will eventually fall apart. The same is true for kids and teenagers. If they grow up with a shallow approach to life, they are likely to self-destruct as they enter adulthood. Isn't it interesting that the very construct we use to protect ourselves and hold it all together is ultimately the thing that can undo us?

A SHALLOW APPROACH TO LIFE CAN ROB LEADERS OF THEIR POTENTIAL TO GIVE A KID OR TEENAGER HOPE. ↓ This

Young people need to grow up knowing they were made in the image of God and loved by Jesus so they can love others. But they may never understand what that looks like in action unless they have a few adults who demonstrate what it means to move beyond The Shallow Way.

So, let's talk about what we mean by shallow. Metaphorically speaking, isn't it simply the opposite of deeper? Certainly. But what does deeper really look like in action?

Recently Reggie and I (Kristen) were speaking at an event in

Northern California and had an opportunity to go to lunch with some of the staff for the event. At the table, someone started a conversation about the characteristic differences between Northern Cal and Southern Cal. They talked about how Los Angeles was for the fashionable, superficial, popular crowd. Things were different in the location where this group lived (essentially, women wore less makeup).

The conversation bounced around the differences until one leader made a witty and insightful remark, "Yeah, in Southern California they're so shallow. They judge you on your appearance. Here we only judge you on your academic achievement." We all laughed. They were right. Masks come in all shapes and sizes, and we are often tempted to correct the shallowness we observe in someone else simply by applying a different shallow mask to ourselves.

Religion has been a friend of The Shallow Way for thousands of years. In church circles, we like to counterbalance the shallowness of culture by claiming we are deeper. But deeper how?

- Deeper in our understanding of theology?
- Deeper in our spiritual practice?
- Deeper in our knowledge of Greek architecture?

In the church, we have a way of making deeper just another version of shallow in disguise. So, what if we need a less ambiguous term for deeper living? What if a clearer alternative to The Shallow Way is learning to be personal?

Think about it.

SHALLOW IS FAST.
PERSONAL TAKES TIME.

SHALLOW IS EASY.
PERSONAL IS COMPLICATED.

SHALLOW IS SAFE.
PERSONAL IS RISKY.

SHALLOW IS CERTAIN.
PERSONAL IS UNRESOLVED.

SHALLOW IS DISMISSIVE.
PERSONAL IS INTERESTED.

SHALLOW IS FAMILIAR.
PERSONAL IS UNPREDICTABLE.

SHALLOW COSTS MONEY.
PERSONAL COSTS ME.

You don't typically have to work at being shallow. But you do have to work at being personal. That's why one of the best things any adult can possibly do is begin to show up consistently in the life of a kid or teenager and be personal.

I (Virginia) am the product of an African American urban church that loved young people. The pastor and leadership team prioritized youth. They saw the church as more than programming. While I was still a young person, the church gave me my first opportunities to lead. They saw something in me the surrounding culture and education system failed to see.

These opportunities were the catalyst I needed to recognize the potential I may have never seen in myself. My greatest memories are conversations with adults who took the time to really know me. They chose to be personally involved in my life, and in doing so they provided a positive voice of hope.

In other environments I was unseen, but at church I was seen. In other places I was overlooked, but the youth leaders saw who I could become. Looking back, I am convinced those leaders nurtured me because they made it personal.

They honored my personal worth.
They respected my personal voice.
They invested in my personal dreams.

That's what happens when you choose to be personal.
All three of us have discovered that as Christian leaders, it's imperative for us to develop authentic relationships and to get closer to the frontlines where kids are hurting.

The result of shallow ministry is disillusionment.
The result of personal ministry is hope.

That's why Jesus showed up in a religiously impersonal culture. He wanted to establish a stark contrast between a personal God and any version of God that portrayed Him as indifferent and disinterested.

JESUS WAS PERSONAL.
HE TOUCHED PEOPLE WHO HAD DISEASES.
HE SPOKE RESPECTFULLY TO A SCANDALOUS WOMAN.
HE WEPT AT THE TOMB OF A FRIEND.
HE BROKE A RULE TO GET SOMEONE OUT OF TROUBLE.
HE MET LEADERS PRIVATELY, IN THE MIDDLE OF THE NIGHT.
HE WASHED THE FEET OF HIS DISCIPLES.
HE INVITED HIMSELF TO A WILD PARTY.
HE PLAYED WITH TODDLERS.

WHY?
BECAUSE JESUS DIDN'T SEE HUMANS THE WAY
THE AVERAGE HUMAN SEES HUMANS.

Jesus . . .
honored those who were disgraced.
befriended those who were marginalized.
embraced those who were rejected.
forgave those who were shunned.
believed in those who were broken.

That kind of sounds like the opposite of shallow living, doesn't it? **Jesus never got so busy trying to save everyone that He didn't stop to help someone.**

The Gospel according to Luke records a well-known story of a wealthy tax collector who had a reputation for cheating people out of their money.[1] One day, the notorious businessman heard that Jesus was passing through his town.

In an attempt to get a glimpse of the famous rabbi, Zacchaeus sprinted ahead of the crowd and scrambled up a tree. It just so happened that when Jesus spotted the man, He stopped and called him out by name in front of everyone. What Jesus did next shocked the entire community. He invited Himself to the tax collector's home to stay the night. Criticism and rumors began to circulate throughout the town.

Why would Jesus show favor to someone like Zacchaeus? How could Jesus not care what this man had done to so many families? What good could come from spending time with the most dishonest man in the community? It was clear when Zacchaeus climbed down from the sycamore tree that no one in the crowd saw him the way Jesus did.

The crowd saw a man who was driven by personal greed.
The crowd saw an individual who would use anybody to get ahead.
The crowd saw someone who had hurt their community.

But not Jesus.
He saw a man with intrinsic worth.
He saw an individual who reflected God's image.
He saw someone with extraordinary potential.

Jesus never let public opinion change the way He saw anyone.

Maybe Jesus chose Zacchaeus in front of everyone to prove what can happen when anyone is treated like someone God loves. Think about this: The way Jesus saw Zacchaeus ultimately changed the way everyone saw Zacchaeus. Better yet, the way Jesus saw Zacchaeus changed the way Zacchaeus saw himself.

Something remarkable happens when you start seeing people

---

1 Luke 19:1-10

the way Jesus sees them. No one imagined how Jesus' personal interaction with one man would change their entire town. But it did. Zacchaeus changed so much that Jesus said, "Today, salvation has come to your house."

JESUS IMPLIED THAT SOMETHING HAD HAPPENED IN THE IMMEDIATE MOMENT OF ZACCHAEUS' LIFE THAT WOULD TRANSFORM EVERY MOMENT OF HIS FUTURE. THAT'S THE EFFECT AN ENCOUNTER WITH JESUS HAS IN SOMEONE'S LIFE.

It's as if He were saying, "You were living an empty, lonely, shallow existence. Now that I'm here, you can start living with a different kind of hope."

We need to remember that the Gospel is personal. If we take our cue from Jesus, we will stop limiting the good news to only what happens after someone dies. It's possible for a personal encounter with Jesus to impact someone's life while they are living. At the end of the Zacchaeus story, Jesus reminds everyone of His mission, "The Son of Man came to seek and save the lost."[2] Some scholars even speculate this is the summative statement for the entire book of Luke.

Zacchaeus had lost his sense of identity
until Jesus called him by name and said, "Come down out of that tree."

Zacchaeus had lost his sense of belonging
until Jesus said, "I'm coming to your house. Let's spend some time together."

Zacchaeus had lost his sense of purpose
until Jesus saw him in a different way than the crowd had seen him.

Then Zacchaeus had HOPE.

Don't miss this.

---

2 Luke 19:10

WHAT JESUS DID FOR ZACCHAEUS WAS PERSONAL.

He pulled Zacchaeus out of the crowd so He could spend time with him individually. Jesus was on the road to Jerusalem to save the world, but He stopped on the way to the cross to save one person and remind the rest of us that the mission is personal.

Jesus' encounter with Zacchaeus is such a powerful example of what it means to be personal we will continue to refer to it throughout this book. But we don't want you to miss the main point:

The church needs more leaders to learn how to be personal because too many kids feel invisible or ignored.

There is an epidemic rise in
bullying,
emotional abuse,
depression,
self-harm, and
suicide among kids and teenagers.[3]

If we think these issues are going to be resolved by
deeper worship songs,
deeper Bible studies, or
deeper theological debates,
then we are actually shallow in our thinking.

It's more important now than ever before to redefine what it means to be deep, and invite a generation of leaders to be more personal.

Remember, the gravitational pull for all of us will always be toward the shallow. We can easily convince ourselves of the need to
add followers,
build a platform,
or teach a lesson,
but none of those things matter if we fail to be personal.

---

3 You don't have to go far to find the latest data on these trends, but to get started, look up the the YouthTruth report on bullying from Hechinger, the Centers for Disease Control and Prevention reports on youth suicide and self-harm, and the Pew Research Center's Social and Demographic Trends.

STOP AND LOOK AROUND.
THERE'S SOMEONE WHO NEEDS YOU TO SEE THEM.

If you look closely, there's a kid who has pushed their way past the crowd into a space where they hope you will notice them. There's a kid who needs someone to see them.

They need you to see the everyday world that is defining them.
They need you to see the private doubts that are paralyzing them.
They need you to see the potential future that is waiting for them.

If you want to move beyond The Shallow Way you may have to become a little more personal.

Think about what Jesus did for Zacchaeus.
Jesus identified Zacchaeus in way that communicated value.
Jesus instinctively addressed what mattered to Zacchaeus.
Jesus took the time to enter into Zacchaeus' everyday world.
Jesus responded to Zacchaeus in a way that removed his shame.
Jesus believed in Zacchaeus' potential to do good.

What if you could do the same for a kid or teenager?

THAT'S WHAT THIS BOOK IS ABOUT.
IT'S A CALL FOR ALL OF US TO . . .
IDENTIFY SOMEONE IN A WAY THAT COMMUNICATES VALUE.
DISCOVER WHAT MATTERS TO SOMEONE TO PROVE THEY MATTER.
TAKE THE TIME TO UNDERSTAND SOMEONE'S EVERYDAY CONTEXT.
RESPOND TO SOMEONE IN A WAY THAT REPLACES SHAME WITH HOPE.
BELIEVE IN SOMEONE'S POTENTIAL TO LIVE A REMARKABLE STORY.

The point is, if you want to be a transformational leader, then it has to be personal. If you want to anchor a kid's faith to something that lasts, then it has to be personal. If you want to offer hope in a world of hopelessness, then it has to be personal.

CHAPTER 2

DO YOU KNOW
MY NAME?

C armen Fariña was an educator in New York City for almost 50 years. She went on to serve as Chancellor for two thousand New York City Schools and as the head of the New York City Department of Education. Reflecting on her career, Fariña recounts how she was born in Brooklyn during the 1950s to parents who fled Spain during the Spanish Civil War. When she entered kindergarten, she was the only non-English-speaking child in her class. Imagine the challenges of trying to integrate into a classroom where no one speaks your language. Not only would you need to learn where to sit, when to raise your hand, and how to ask permission to go to the bathroom, you would have to learn to do this with an entirely new language.

One day Fariña's father got a postcard from the school indicating his child had been absent for six weeks. As a father who had personally taken his daughter to class each morning, he was confused. So, he went back to the school and asked, "Why don't you know my daughter is here every day?" Fariña's teacher responded: "I can't pronounce her last name and she doesn't answer to the name I gave her."

Carmen Fariña, who eventually became the first in her family to graduate from college, was marked absent not based on her attendance, but based on one teacher's approach to calling roll.

This event shaped Fariña's personal strategy as an educator. During the keynote address at the National Association for Bilingual Education, Fariña said this:

"Mispronouncing a student's name essentially renders that student invisible. A promise I give to every parent in New York City is your child will be spoken to by the name you give them, not the name someone else gives them."[1]

Have you ever considered this thought?
How you say someone's name can be personal or shallow.

We say names in a flippant way all the time.
But have you ever thought about what
a careless tone,
a dismissive look, or
a lazy pronunciation
actually communicates?

You are probably thinking, "Yeah, but I'm not very good with names." Neither are we. But, there's significance to a name. It's part of someone's identity. When we dismiss a person's name we forfeit their trust to become more personal. Most people care more than they will admit when someone doesn't take the time to learn and remember their name.

Maybe that's why Jesus called Zacchaeus by name.

Imagine again what it must have been like for Zacchaeus as he

---

1 "Chancellor Carmen Farina's Remarks at the National Association for Bilingual Education Conference," Accessed 7 April 2019, https://www.schools.nyc.gov/about-us/news/announcements/contentdetails/2016/03/03/chancellor-carmen-fariña-s-remarks-at-the-national-association-for-bilingual-education-conference

rounded the corner in Jericho to see the gathering crowd. Think about the rumors that might have been passing excitedly from one person to another.

"My cousin Mary told me that He fed a crowd of thousands with only five loaves and two fish."

"That's nothing. My nephew told me when Jesus visited his village He stopped to talk with people with leprosy and after He spent time with them, they went to see the priests and their leprosy was gone!"

Maybe these rumors sparked hope in Zacchaeus. He knew first-hand that no one hung out with tax collectors. Everyone saw them as avaricious and dishonest—and maybe that was true. They did bring in a sizable income by demanding more tax than Rome required and then keeping the excess.

As chief tax collector for all Jericho, Zacchaeus had not only experienced isolation, but had seen its effects on other tax collectors who worked for him. No one likes a cheat. But if these rumors were true, Jesus was a man who spent time with lepers. And lepers didn't usually get many visitors either.

Imagine Zacchaeus pushing ahead to look for a spot with a view. Across the road he sees an opening and makes a move in that direction. The lady to his left steps sideways blocking his path with a disgusted look. Sighing, he walks a little further into the crowd. He notices a second gap with a clear view of the street and moves toward it. But before he gets there a tall man steps into his path. "What are you doing here?" he sneers. "Go home, little man."

Maybe Zacchaeus was tempted to turn around. There's something about a crowd of people that makes loneliness even more poignant.

He was standing in the street surrounded by the people he cheated.

But Luke tells us Zacchaeus didn't turn back. He ran ahead and climbed a tree. Isn't it hard not to wonder what motivated that decision? Surely climbing trees wasn't an adult hobby. Maybe he hadn't climbed a tree since he was a little boy. But throwing all dignity aside, he climbs. Twenty, maybe thirty feet into the air, he climbs. Surely this is not the proudest moment of Zacchaeus' life.

Can you imagine the internal monologue?

"Zacchaeus, look at yourself. People hate you. You don't even like yourself. And here you are, a grown man—well, not that grown, let's be honest—but you're climbing a tree like a child."

Then Jesus spoke.
"Zacchaeus."

"Zacchaeus."
Jesus looked at him and said his name.

We could speculate on how Jesus knew Zacchaeus' name. Maybe he had heard about him. Zacchaeus was obviously one of the most hated guys in town.

How many short greedy rich men could there be in Jericho? Perhaps Jesus just assumed, "I bet that's the guy who's taking everybody's money."

Or then again, it could have been that Jesus just knew Zacchaeus' name because He was Jesus. Do you ever wonder how many times Jesus played the God-card? He could have a little bit of fun walking down the road, calling people by name even though He had never met them.

"Oh, hey John, how's Deborah doing? When's the wedding?"
"Hey Sarah, so sorry your dog got run over by that chariot."
"Hey Alex, how's that back pain? I bet it's not hurting now, is it?"

But what if Jesus said Zacchaeus' name for another reason? Not because Zacchaeus had a reputation that preceded him even outside of Jericho. Not that Jesus enjoyed showing off. What if Jesus simply knew the power of saying someone's name out loud?

Zacchaeus must have been surprised to hear his name—especially when it was spoken in a positive way by someone like Jesus. Imagine the flood of emotions that suddenly erupted in Zacchaeus' brain.

"That's me."
"That's me and everybody heard that it's me."
"That's me and it's Jesus talking to me."
"That's me and He is actually interested in getting to know me."

What a day-changing moment.

WHEN JESUS SAID ZACCHAEUS' NAME JESUS MODELED **HONOR**.

Jesus recognized Zacchaeus in front of a crowd of people who had every right to dishonor and discredit him. Jesus seized a powerful opportunity to leverage one word to make a meaningful and honorable statement to Zacchaeus.

Have you ever thought about how long it takes to say someone's name? In a split second, Jesus said one word that affected Zacchaeus' sense of identity, belonging, and purpose.

With one word, Jesus reminded the crowd that this man was not a position, "chief tax collector," but a person, "Zacchaeus." Can you imagine what this might look like for kids and teenagers who live in a world of labels?

Rich kid
Poor kid
Popular girl
Athlete
Smart kid
Nerd
Gamer

Too many of us underestimate the power of someone's name. It's often the first word anyone learns to recognize, speak, or write.

Research consistently reveals a sudden rise in a person's brain activity in response to his or her own name. In fact, comparative brain imaging indicates that our brains respond differently to our own name than they would to any other name or sound. This is even true for infants in the first nine months of life. It's as if a person's brain lights up with the response, "That's me!"[2]

I (Virginia) had a bad habit of confusing the name of my son's current girlfriend with the names of his former girlfriends. (What can I say? He was popular!) Calling Tiffany "Tamara" the first few times definitely made for a few awkward encounters. But my son said it definitely upped his game when I took the time to learn the correct name of the girl sitting beside him at the dinner table.

I (Kristen) had the privilege of attending three years of high school under the leadership of an extraordinary principal named Jenny Springer.

One of the many things that set Dr. Springer apart was the way she intentionally learned every student's name. Twenty years later, I watch in admiration as she continues to recognize former students by name, and how those students consistently share the way she influenced their stories.

In every area of life, we can be better leaders, communicators, parents, friends, and volunteers if we know people's names. Developing a skill of remembering a name is even more important if you work with kids and teenagers. And as simple as it sounds, pronunciation and spelling matter.

Admit it: When a barista carelessly misspells your name on your double latte, there's a slight disconnect. If a server pauses to ask how to correctly say your name, you might smile.

The Santa Clara County Office of Education recognized the importance of correctly pronouncing a child's name and raised

---

2 Dennis P. Carmody, Michael Lewis "Brain activation when hearing one's own and others' names," *Brain Research*. Elsevier. Accessed 20 Oct 2006 at https://doi.org/10.1016/j. brainres.2006.07.121 .

awareness at a national level through the "My Name, My Identity" campaign. Similar to Carmen Fariña's experience, the campaign focuses on the cultural awareness involved in honoring the names of children of all ethnic backgrounds.

They challenge students to take a pledge to respect others by pronouncing each others' names correctly. According to these leaders, when you start correctly saying someone's name, "you can foster a sense of belonging and build positive relationships in the classroom, which are crucial for healthy social, psychological, and educational outcomes."[3]

Can you imagine what it would communicate if we took the same pledge as leaders and volunteers?

My father (Virginia) served as a lead pastor of a church for many years. One day I was looking through one of my father's books and noticed a piece of paper inside that said, "Know and learn the name of each person." As a pastor, he recognized that knowing someone's name is personal.

And it wasn't confined to the church. I noticed he took the time to remember the names of the cashier at the local supermarket and the neighborhood sub shop. He communicated value with each encounter by addressing people by their names.

WHEN YOU SAY SOMEONE'S NAME,
you are doing much more than just saying their name. You are making a statement about a person's existence, purpose, and value.

WHEN YOU SAY SOMEONE'S NAME,
you are saying someone is worth remembering. Chances are it's much more important than you realize. It may even be more important than they realize.

Maybe you won't hear a fourth grader say, "Thank you so much for remembering my name. I will never be the same because you pronounced it right!" But that doesn't mean they didn't notice.

---

3 https://www.mynamemyidentity.org

WHEN YOU SAY SOMEONE'S NAME, you silently communicate an answer to a number of underlying questions like . . .

Do you notice when I'm there? Or not there?

Do you like being around me?

Do you recognize my uniqueness?

Saying a kid or teenager's name won't change their everyday reality, but it could give them just enough hope to believe they are worth remembering.

In the split second it takes to look at them and say their name, you can give a kid an emotional nudge in a positive direction.

> **SO START DOING WHAT JESUS DID FOR ZACCHAEUS. LEARN HOW TO IDENTIFY SOMEONE IN A WAY THAT COMMUNICATES VALUE.**

What would it take for you to get in the habit of learning and remembering someone's name? Okay. You're not Jesus. You and I don't have the God advantage of supernaturally knowing everyone's name. We have to work pretty hard sometimes to get it right. A name is just one more piece of information. It's one more thing to remember and recall in addition to appointments, deadlines, tasks, and every other piece of information we need to keep our adult world together. So here are some practical tips to learn and remember someone's name.

SAY THE NAME OUT LOUD

Immediately say the name back aloud when someone tells you his or her name. That helps log it into your brain. Say it again while you are continuing the conversation. That's just good practice. Say it whenever you greet them later so it's obvious that you remember. Say it when you want to introduce someone else into the conversation. Research shows that humans never get tired of hearing their own name . . . at least their brains don't.[4] So say someone's name often and out loud.

PRONOUNCE THE NAME CORRECTLY

Practice saying the name exactly. If the individual has a self-chosen name that differs from what's on your attendance sheet, it's okay to go with "Bobby" instead of "Robert." If the pronunciation is challenging, it's okay to ask for help. Just be sensitive about how you ask. Educator and researcher Rita Kohli explains two approaches to how an adult responds to a challenging name. "It matters what you do when you're in front of a child and struggling with their name. Is it framed as my inability to say someone's name, or is it framed as the student doing something to make your life more difficult?"[5] Repeat the name until you get it right. Pronouncing a kid's name correctly communicates respect for their history, family, and culture. It will matter to them that it matters to you.

DISCOVER THE NAME'S STORY

Many names have a story. If you really want to get personal, discover more about the story behind a kid or teenager's name. You may hear a wildly fascinating story about their great aunt Florence. Or you may learn that their name has a significant or symbolic meaning. In many cultures a name denotes tradition or family history. Taking the time to ask questions about the origin of a name can give you insight into their culture. You may even find that a kid has never heard the story of his or her name and you could prompt a little mutual discovery for you both. The more you understand the story of a name, the more insight you will have into a kid's story.

---

4 Cherry EC. "Some experiments on the recognition of speech, with one and two ears," *Journal of the Acoustical Society of America*. 1953;25:975–979. (One noteworthy exception: Our unscientific observation of female humans raising children indicates they DO however get tired of hearing the word, "Mom.")

5 "A Teacher Mispronouncing a Student's Name Can Have a Lasting Impact," *PBS NewsHour*, Accessed 10 April 2019 https://www.pbs.org/newshour/education/a-teacher-mispronouncing-a-students-name-can-have-a-lasting-impact

WRITE THE NAME DOWN SOMEWHERE

Writing a name with a pen and paper, with a marker and notecard, or with a crayon on the back of an activity sheet often makes it easier to remember. Some leaders may choose to also type the name into the notes app on their phone for easy accessibility. Either way, if you want to remember someone's name, you need to log it somewhere where you can reference it occasionally.

I (Virginia) will never forget one evening when a student whose name I kept messing up shouted out, "That's not my name!" Then she pronounced it correctly for me. I was a bit embarrassed but I made a point to write her name out phonetically in order to not make that mistake again. Consider writing each name at least two ways: first with the correct spelling, then with the name spelled out phonetically, so you can remember how to pronounce it later.

CONNECT THE NAME VISUALLY

For years, I (Reggie) have led an orientation for college interns working at summer camps for teenagers. Before our first meeting, I always create flash cards with the names and faces of each intern. I love the feeling of greeting every intern by name when they walk in the door for the first meeting.

I (Kristen) led small groups of teenage girls for over a decade. Since I often struggle to remember names, I developed the habit of writing the names of each girl in a circle that represented where they sat. This practice helped me connect faces to names and even recall important parts of our conversations.

Anything you can do to connect to their name visually will make a stronger imprint in your memory. One free resource we've created to help leaders store information they need to know is the Lead Small app. Once you store a name electronically in the app, it's easy to add the names of parents, pets, and interests.

We will talk more about those categories in the next chapters. But for now start with visually connecting someone's name to his or her face.

PRAY THE NAME FREQUENTLY

Here's an interesting idea. Praying for people doesn't change how God sees people; it changes how we see people. Praying privately for someone (by name) will affect how you see that individual. Praying publically for someone (by name) will affect how they see themselves.

I (Reggie) remember the first time I heard someone pray my name. I was seven years old when I walked passed the bedroom of an elderly aunt who had adopted my mom as a child. Through the open door, I heard her say my name in her prayer. I quietly stopped and listened. It forever changed the way I saw God, myself, and even her.

What if one of the best ways to move from shallow to personal is to begin a habit of praying for somebody you know by name?

Maybe you could set a reminder in your phone for a certain time of day. Maybe create a prayer calendar so you can pray for a few people each day or week. You might be surprised at how it changes you and them.

LEARNING SOMEONE'S NAME IS AN IMPORTANT FIRST STEP IN BEING PERSONAL.

It matters *if* you say someone's name.
It matters *how* you say someone's name.
It matters *how* often you say someone's name.

In a world where so many kids are known by
a number on a jersey,
digits on a carpool tag,
random usernames,
and national statistics,
we need more caring adults who know them personally. By name.

What if you simply decided to surprise someone today by using their name correctly?

Whether you realize it or not, there is a kid or teenager stuck in a tree looking for someone who will stop. They are quietly wondering, "Is there anyone out there who will . . .
acknowledge me?
remember me?
connect with me?
engage me?"

If you want to live the kind of life that gives hope, begin by knowing a few names. Everybody needs somebody who knows their name.

DO YOU KNOW
MY NAME?

WHEN YOU KNOW MY NAME YOU MODEL HONOR, *SO I HAVE HOPE THAT I AM* WORTH REMEMBERING.

Identify someone in a way that communicates value

IT'S PERSONAL

CHAPTER 3

DO YOU KNOW
WHAT MATTERS TO ME?

Trucks matter. At least they seem to matter to kids. Ask Tonka. Since 1964, they have sold 16 million toy dump trucks.

Have you ever watched a three-year-old's eyes light up when he or she sees a toy truck? There's something about a good set of wheels that seems to capture the imagination.

Trucks also matter to teenagers—or at least some of them. I (Reggie) recently learned that pick-up trucks matter in most small towns in Georgia. I volunteer to work with teenagers in a rural community a few times each month, and I've learned the pick-up truck of choice is the F-150. At least that's the truck guys around town post about the most.

Every Sunday evening we have a youth program we call "High School Gathering." Recently, a few of the guys stopped coming as frequently. When one of the leaders asked them why they hadn't shown up in a few weeks, their answer caught me off-guard, "We'll come back if we can hang out in our trucks in the parking lot."

Evidently, some leaders were nervous when they noticed teenagers lingering in the parking lot after the gathering. So they responsibly suggested that it was probably a good idea to move on. I guess no one realized how much trucks mattered.

It made sense to be cautious. Some teenage guys might claim . . .
girls matter,
beer matters,
and vaping matters.

The combination of trucks with any of those things in a dark parking lot could be problematic. But no one stopped to think trucks might matter so much they would be reason enough to stop coming to High School Gathering.

IF YOU WANT TO BE MORE PERSONAL,
YOU HAVE TO TAKE TIME TO UNDERSTAND WHAT REALLY
MATTERS TO SOMEONE. AND IN ORDER TO DO THAT,
YOU HAVE TO UNDERSTAND WHY IT MATTERS.

When it came to giving the teenagers of Wrightsville, Georgia, a place to belong— a place to find hope—we needed to go along with how much trucks matter simply because . . .
fun matters.
friends matter.
conversation matters.

Which is why we decided that maybe as long as there's a leader in the parking lot to monitor activity, it's okay for trucks to matter.

Maybe trucks don't really matter to the kids you lead.

Maybe in your community . . .
unicorns matter.
belt bags matter.
K-pop matters.
homecoming matters.
Nike shoes matter.
slime matters.
chocolate donuts matter.
Play-Doh matters.
Instagram matters.
Fortnite matters.
pepperoni pizza matters.
Marvel movies matter.

But no matter where you live, and no matter who you lead, this part is always true: What matters to someone *actually matters*. And when you take the time to figure out what matters to kids and teenagers, they begin to believe *they* matter too.

If you are going to shift from shallow living to becoming more personal, you have to become interested in something that interests someone else.

That shift won't happen automatically. It takes a degree of intentionality. You might not naturally feel intrigued by what's happening on Fortnite or what someone-you've-never-met said on their Finstagram last week.[1]

Sometimes you have to deliberately disrupt your present schedule to remind everyone, including yourself, that being personal requires paying attention. That's what Jesus did in the story of Zacchaeus.

Consider for a minute what was happening in Jesus's life on the day He encountered Zacchaeus. Let's step back to before the moment Jesus said Zacchaeus' name and examine the context

---

1 Youth Culture changes rapidly. At the time we are writing, Fortnite is a popular video game, and it is the common practice of many young people to have a second, unofficial Instagram account they refer to as a Finstagram account.

surrounding what happened that day on the road into Jericho.

Imagine this.
Jesus is at the height of His popularity.
He's steadily gaining followers.
He's had a few sermons go viral.
His Transjordan tour has been wildly successful.
And He's the center of national controversy.

Of course, for Jesus this is about much more than growing the largest Palestinian platform. He's about to embark on the pivotal moment of His life—actually the pivotal moment of all of human history.

Jesus knows what no one else does. He's on the road, literally, to do great things. This seemingly small interaction with Zacchaeus is the last recorded personal encounter Jesus has before He dies.

So here He is. The Savior. The Messiah. Entering Jericho on His way to Jerusalem where He will be welcomed with palm branches and shouts of "Hosanna." He's fulfilled prophecies, worked miracles, and spent years discipling a few men so that hopefully they understand what's about to happen.

As He walks the road into New Jericho, Jesus can see the palace of Herod the Great, the same ruler who ordered the slaughter of infants when he learned of Jesus' birth. He can see shepherds driving spring sheep on their way to Jerusalem in preparation for Passover. Maybe His heart begins to race a little. Surely, He must be thinking about His forthcoming encounters with Antipas, Pilate, and the governing officials. Jesus' moment approaches. Like Frodo entering Mordor, or Harry Potter returning to Hogwarts for one final battle, Jesus is nearing Jerusalem.

THEN ONE SMALL MAN CLIMBS A TREE.

If anyone could have made the argument, "I don't really have time for you," it would be Jesus in this moment. But Luke records a different story.

"When Jesus reached the spot, He looked up."

Can't you just imagine the disciples traveling with Jesus? A few of them keep walking unaware that anything has happened. Those who are walking behind Jesus cast an awkward glance at each other as if to say, "Oh, are we stopping for something?"

Perhaps Peter and Andrew notice Zacchaeus and wish they could run interference for Jesus. If they could just ask this guy to please get off the tree, to step away from the road, to back off and let the Messiah pass. But they must have fought off their instincts, knowing how Jesus was about these things. Only a short time earlier Jesus had scolded them for trying to keep some snotty toddlers off His lap.

Maybe James looked a little deeper and took in this man's rich clothing and well-kept beard. It must have been obvious that this man had money. Here was one more guy like the rich young ruler.

But Jesus noticed something else. He saw a man alone in a crowd. So alone, in fact, that he had climbed a tree. It seems likely that Jesus saw something about Zacchaeus beyond his physical stature, his geographical location, or his wealthy appearance.

He saw Zacchaeus' heart.
He knew what mattered to Zacchaeus.
And He knew that Zacchaeus really mattered.

WHEN JESUS STOPPED FOR ZACCHAEUS
JESUS MODELED **FRIENDSHIP.**

Friendship is never convenient or easy. It almost always requires us to stop what we are doing–even when what we are doing is very important.

In the middle of His mission to save the world,
in front of the whole town of Jericho,
in spite of the critics,

Jesus stopped.

Earlier in His ministry, Jesus told a story about a man walking the road from Jericho to Jerusalem—the same road He and His followers were about to take. In that parable Jesus explained what it means to love your neighbor in terms that clearly implied the importance of stopping for someone else.[2]

Shallow leaders have a tendency to
keep moving too fast,
avoid personal interruptions,
and never learn how to see the kids who are climbing trees.

WHEN JESUS STOPPED AND SHOWED INTEREST IN ZACCHAEUS, HE VALIDATED ZACCHAEUS' **WORTH.**

Showing interest in someone's interests builds a relationship. I (Kristen) absolutely detest small talk. I don't know if it's because I'm an introvert or because I just lack patience, but there's something about carrying on a 30-minute conversation about last week's game that makes me want to run screaming from the room. Ironically, my temptation to cut the conversation short and make an exit is actually pretty shallow.

Sometimes we all need to pause and engage in seemingly small conversations. That may be especially true when the conversation is about something that interests someone else. When you make it a habit to discover another person's interests, they become more interesting to you. And when you pause to discover another person's interests, you will actually become more interesting.

If you want to move from shallow living to becoming more personal, never underestimate the importance of the small stuff. Pausing your adult schedule long enough to explore the interests of a second-grader will never feel very heroic. Setting aside time to eat a Big Mac and fries with a seventh-grader, only to have him spend the entire hour showing you YouTube videos of someone else playing video games may not feel very significant.

---

2 Luke 10:25-37, The Parable of The Good Samaritan

But if you don't discipline yourself to stop and discover what interests those around you, chances are you will never get very personal. And if you don't become personal, you will never develop the kind of trusting relationship that is required to navigate bigger life circumstances.

A few years ago I (Kristen) had an opportunity to interview over a dozen professional counselors who work with children and adolescents. I hosted three separate one-day meetings to discuss kids in crisis: how to recognize crisis and what to do when crisis was suspected. One of the interesting points that arose through these conversations was the absolute necessity for every kid to have a consistent adult who really knew their interests.

Consider this. The more familiar you are with someone's interests, the easier it will be for you to know when they actually need your help.

If you know a kid's interests, you will stand a better chance of knowing when . . .
their interests are controlling them.
their interests are being suppressed.
they have lost interest.

All three of these scenarios suggest a kid is up a tree. What my conversations with family counselors taught me is this: Adults often fail to recognize a kid in crisis unless they have already invested enough consistent time to know that child well.

It's hard to talk a kid down out of tree, if you have no idea why she climbed it in the first place.

> **YOU BEGIN TO KNOW
> SOMEONE WHEN YOU**
> DISCOVER SOMEONE'S INTERESTS
> TO VALIDATE THEIR WORTH.

Kids and teenagers often feel invisible. They need adults who will pause long enough to discover their interests to prove to them that they are interesting. They need adults who will take the time to really see who they are and who they are becoming.

When you engage in someone's interests you silently communicate an answer to a number of underlying questions like . . .

Do you know what I enjoy doing?
Do you know what makes me laugh?
Do you know what I'm afraid of?

When you recall someone's interests, you are saying, "You are worth the time it takes to discover you." Better yet, when you learn to appreciate what someone else likes, you are actually suggesting, "You are worth liking."

If learning someone's name is a way to prove they are worth remembering, then discovering someone's interests is a way to show they are worth liking.

If you are leading more than one kid or teenager, you may gravitate toward the interests of kids who are similar to you. But remember, the way you demonstrate interest in a kid's interests communicates something about that kid's worth.

Never marginalize the interests of kids who . . .
don't conform to social trends.
don't fit gender stereotypes.
don't assimilate to the dominant culture of their community.

There's a tendency to want to redirect the interests of . . .
the first grade kid who recites movies
the fourth grade boy who likes to paint
the seventh grade girl who talks about her Rubik's Cube
the ninth grade guy who makes sushi
the eleventh grade girl who collects old Tamagotchis
rather than welcoming these interests with mutual fascination.

There's something in us that wants to do that kid a favor. We tend to assume if we could just help them become interested in things that were a little more socially acceptable they would have more friends. We convince ourselves we are trying to help.

That kind of help is shallow.

When you help a kid by trying to redirect their interests to something that makes you or others more comfortable you send the wrong message. Instead of saying, "You are interesting, valuable, and likeable," you instead communicate, "You make us uncomfortable. If you want to belong, you need to change yourself first."

Kids and teenagers are quick to pick up on our signals about norms. After all, a large portion of childhood and adolescence is about learning how humans behave. But when we signal that a kid's interests are somehow unacceptable, they begin to shut down the things that make them feel alive.

Over time, kids can learn to conform so well that they lose touch with the imaginative, creative, expressive things that used to give them hope.

Discovering the interests of a preschooler may require some patience. Discovering the interests of an elementary aged kid may require some humility. And discovering the interests of a teenager may require some perseverance. But you can do this. Here are a few suggestions to help you discover what really matters.

PAY ATTENTION TO THE CLUES

Young people often drop clues about what really matters to them. But if you aren't paying attention, the clues are easy to miss. If you want to discover their interests, you may need to listen more than you talk.
Listen to what music they want to play.
Listen for who they talk about following on social media.
Listen to their body language when they walk into a room.

I (Virginia) discovered many years ago that the way you ask, "How was your week?" can be shallow or personal. During a youth ministry hangout at my house, a student came into the kitchen to help. When I inquired about her day she gave me a here-is-the-answer-you-want-to-hear response. I could tell from her body language she was holding back, and then I realized that it probably wasn't typical for a high school girl to leave her friends and choose to come help in the kitchen.

When I pressed for more information, she said, "Oh, you are going to make me go to the place of my pain?" The conversation that followed opened the door to a new level in our relationship. When she realized that I was genuinely interested in her answer to my question, she knew she could trust me with a more genuine response.

ASK CLARIFYING QUESTIONS

Be careful not to confuse *what a person does* with a person's interests. Just because a kid plays Little League doesn't mean he is interested in baseball; he might just like the snacks. Just because a girl plays lacrosse doesn't mean she's interested in sports; she might just enjoy time with the other girls on the team. We had one small group leader tell us, "My middle school girls like K-pop and it has nothing to do with the music. They just like Korean boys." The only way to really understand a kid's interests may be to ask some questions like, "How do you feel about math league?" Or "What is it about cooking that you enjoy?"

CONSIDER THEIR PERSPECTIVE

It's been a long time since you were a three-year-old. You may have forgotten what it's like to depend on someone else to choose what you will wear for the day, decide what you are eating for breakfast, and take you where you need to go (like the potty). Whether you work with seven-year-olds or 17-year-olds, you may have to step back from your adult world and reimagine life from a different perspective.

It doesn't hurt to study a little child or adolescent development. Learn about personality types. Read about cultural realities that affect the interests of the kids and teenagers you know. Train yourself to consider their interests from their perspective rather than your own.

KNOW WHO THEY KNOW

If you want to know what matters to a kid or teenager, it's simple: People. People always matter to people. The trick is to discover which people really matter. So listen to see if you can discover the answer. Which friends do they talk about most? Which friends have they stopped talking about? Which coaches, mentors, teachers, or family members come up casually in conversation? We will talk more about the importance of knowing *who* matters in the next chapter. For now, we simply recommend writing down the names of the people a kid talks about most.

ENGAGE IN WHAT INTERESTS THEM

One of the most fun ways to discover someone's interests is to actually participate in them together. Sure, maybe karaoke isn't really your thing. Or maybe you've never seen a sticker puzzle. But when you let someone introduce you to something they are interested in, and you participate with them, you may discover a new interest.

Sometimes you won't. Sometimes you will listen to the song they want to share with you and not understand a single lyric. That's okay, too. You don't have to pretend to enjoy every interest. Remember that most interests are fluid. They change as kids grow up and enter new phases. When you show up for kids and teenagers you will never be finished with the work of discovering their interests.

Just remember this. The way you invest energy in discovering a kid's interests is also modeling their value to everyone who is watching.

That's what Jesus did to the astonishment of the crowd when He stopped under the sycamore tree for Zacchaeus. He redefined friendship in a radical way. He offered His companionship to a man no one believed deserved it.

We suspect that Jesus paused for Zacchaeus because Jesus saw something about Zacchaeus' interests that the crowd failed to see. The crowd saw someone who greedily took money beyond what was required. The crowd saw someone who hoarded nice things for himself. The crowd had every reason to assume what mattered to Zacchaeus was wealth.

But Jesus saw a grown man who had run ahead of the crowd to climb a tree. He saw someone who was so interested in meeting the rumored Messiah that he threw all dignity and pretense aside. Jesus saw a man desperately interested in finding hope.

BECAUSE JESUS KNEW WHAT REALLY MATTERED TO ZACCHAEUS, HE STOPPED TO ENGAGE IN ZACCHAEUS' INTEREST.

Look around. Is there someone up a tree waiting for you to stop? If so, what you do in that moment could change something in that person's future. When you pause to show interest, it has the potential to give a kid or teenager hope.

All it takes is for you to be personal enough to communicate:
What matters to you matters to me.
You matter to me.

DO YOU KNOW WHAT MATTERS TO ME?

*WHEN YOU KNOW WHAT I LIKE YOU MODEL FRIENDSHIP,
SO I HAVE HOPE THAT I AM WORTH LIKING.*

Discover someone's interests to validate worth

IT'S PERSONAL

CHAPTER 4

DO YOU KNOW
WHERE I LIVE?

From a window in an office where I (Kristen) work, I can see neighborhood kids walking to the local elementary and middle schools most mornings. It takes less than ten minutes for the average kid to walk down the sidewalk of this suburban community—past a few homes, a couple of restaurants, and a line of trees into their homeroom class. Georgia weather is relatively mild. There are only about 10 days a year when the temperature drops below freezing. Atlanta averages about one inch of snow per year, and even the threat of snow closes schools. So, walking to school where we live is kind of like a walk in the park on a sunny day.

As a former high school teacher, I learned to never assume the trip from home to school is the same for every kid. The events that happen between the time kids wake up and when they walk into the classroom can be extremely varied. Good teachers look for verbal and non-verbal indicators about a kid's emotional state as they enter the classroom, because they know the more they understand a kid's context the more effective they will be at teaching.

In Boston, the average snowfall per year is about 43 inches. A few inches of snow stay on the ground for most days of the winter. I (Virginia) am a little astonished when my Atlanta friends talk about school closings whenever there's a possible snow flurry. Snow, ice, and freezing temperatures are constants in a Boston winter. But there's something else that is true inside the city limits. The route to school can be treacherous, even when the weather is warm and the sun is shining. Educators, mentors, and leaders learn quickly to never assume they really understand what the average kid has witnessed or experienced by the time they get to school. There is a direct correlation to what a kid experiences on his way to school and how he or she behaves at school.

My (Reggie's) dad lied to me when I was a kid growing up. He gave me the "I walked to school everyday barefoot through the snow" speech more than once. Considering the fact that he grew up on a farm in rural South Georgia, he must have simply confused red clay with snow—unless he grew up in the ice age, which is a possibility. Dad did live in rather poor conditions. He was born during the last few years of the Great Depression and was raised in a small house on a cotton farm. We grew up in different cultures at different times. So, it would be a mistake to assume that we understood each other simply because we share similar DNA and we lived in a house together for nearly twenty years.

The point is this. It's presumptuous for anyone to say they understand someone if they don't really know anything about their generational, geographical, or cultural context.

One of the best ways to get to know someone's context is to know where they live. Maybe that's why Jesus' first inclination was to invite Himself to Zaccheus' house. That's a bold move. And it's about as personal as it gets.

Imagine again, the crowd of people gathered on the road to

Jericho. All eyes are on Jesus, as He calls up into the sycamore tree.

"Zacchaeus, come down immediately."

"*Wait*," Zacchaeus must have thought. "*Come down now? As in, you want me to climb back out of this tree with everyone watching?*"

Zacchaeus had climbed the sycamore tree to see Jesus, not to be seen *by* Jesus—and certainly not to be seen by the crowd. But now every eye turned to look up into the leafy branches. That brief exultation Zacchaeus felt when Jesus said his name quickly turned into a kind of heat that coursed through his body and turned his face the color of a red desert rose.

He hadn't realized until now just how comfortable it had been sitting slightly hidden behind the foliage. Nor had he realized when he swung quickly up the tree how much more challenging it was going to be backing himself down out of the tree. Zacchaeus felt suddenly self-aware of his white artisan linen, knee-length tunic, and trunk-slipping sandals, and wished everyone would turn away.

Still, Jesus knew his name.
Jesus said, "Come down."
So down he came.

As Zacchaeus' feet touched the earth, he breathed a sigh of relief. The worst was over. It would probably be a few years before he tried tree-climbing again. He brushed his hands together to shake off the fragments of bark. Then, resolutely not thinking about the on-looking crowd, he looked into Jesus' face.

Jesus smiled and the lines around His eyes wrinkled as if He enjoyed what He'd just seen. "I must stay at your house today."

For a second time, Zacchaeus paused. "*Stay at my house?*"

Immediately an image of his home as he had left it that morning flashed into Zacchaeus' mind. *"When I left today I wasn't expecting to have a guest like Jesus. Have the servants cleaned the chamber pots? I don't remember if I put away those new robes or left them lying on the couch, I was in such a hurry."* But even as he thought these things, Zacchaeus looked into Jesus's face and knew there was no turning back now.

He must have managed to say something in return because before he knew it, Zacchaeus found himself walking straight through the crowd of onlookers leading the way for Jesus and his friends.

It was a beautiful spring day in Jericho. The rainy season was over, and the barley fields were ripe for harvest. And as the sun warmed the pools and glinted off the newly budding green gardens, the knot in Zacchaeus' chest relaxed.

Jesus had defied all social norms to invite Himself to Zacchaeus' home, and Zacchaeus suddenly realized he wasn't worried about Jesus' perception of his house. So what if he had gone a little overboard on sofas last year and his garden was almost obnoxious in its display of exotic imported plants? None of it mattered now.

What mattered was simply that Jesus knew him—home and all.

WHEN JESUS WENT TO ZACCHAEUS'S HOUSE, JESUS MODELED **EMPATHY**.

We define empathy as "pausing your own interests and opinions long enough to discover someone else's interests and opinions." Jesus didn't need to do much discovering. Jesus already knew everything there was to know about Zacchaeus because He knows everything. It comes with being God. Jesus had a primary empathic advantage. But Jesus knew that when He visited Zacchaeus' home, Zacchaeus would probably feel known in a different way.

There's a difference between Jesus and you. There's a lot you don't know. It comes with being human. Although all humans experience similar emotions, we often mistranslate other humans. As individuals, you and I are limited to our own personal experiences. Since our experiences tend to define how we see most things, we often assume that how we see the world is how sensible, reasonable people should see the world.

IF WE WERE ALL REALLY HONEST,
WE MIGHT ADMIT THAT SOMETIMES . . .
WE ASSUME YOU SHOULD FEEL LIKE I FEEL.
WE ASSUME YOU SHOULD THINK LIKE I THINK.
WE ASSUME YOU SHOULD BELIEVE LIKE I BELIEVE.

And when you don't see things my way . . .
I assume you're wrong.
I probably even assume I'm right about why you are wrong.
It rarely occurs to me that I could possibly be wrong about you.

We all have a tendency to superimpose our ideas and story onto the people around us in a way that's not healthy. But that's a shallow approach to relationships that makes people tend to disappear. It's like we are saying, "Your ideas, opinions, and feelings are invisible."

By the way, the majority of those in the crowd assumed they were right about Zacchaeus. But they were wrong. They even assumed Jesus was wrong about His decision to go to Zacchaeus' house. But Jesus was about to teach them a powerful lesson about assumptions.

What would the world look like if we all simply stopped assuming? What would happen if you and I became aware of what we don't know? If I came to your house, and you came to mine, what would it change about how we understand each other?

The 1996 movie *A Time to Kill* has a powerful illustration of this concept. Jake Tyler, a young, white defense lawyer in Mississippi, takes the case to defend Carl Lee Hailey, a black man accused of murdering two white men who raped his ten-year-old-daughter. Near the end of the trial, after enduring threats from the local

Klansmen along with well-intentioned cautions from friends and co-workers, Jake makes an assumption about his relationship with Carl Lee. "Carl Lee, I'm your friend," he claims in a somewhat defensive posture. "We ain't no friends, Jake," Carl Lee responds. "We are on different sides of the line. I ain't never seen you in my part of town. I bet you don't even know where I live. Our daughters, Jake; they ain't never gonna play together."

Carl Lee understood what Jake Tyler failed to see. Until you spend time in someone else's context, you will never be personal.

Similar to Jake Tyler, there's an additional danger for those of us who have grown up watching movies like *A Time to Kill*. It's easy to fool ourselves into believing we have been in contexts when we haven't. We simply make the assumption that if we've read about someone in a book, watched a series on TV, seen a scene in a movie, or listened to a podcast interview, we know everything there is to know about being . . .

white
black
Asian
Latino
male
female
or any number of contextual qualifiers.

Stories help us empathize with people who are different than us. But stories alone can never do what becoming personal will do. Becoming personal will help you understand someone's perspective in a much deeper way.

It may be uncomfortable to immerse yourself in someone else's world. You might encounter different languages, different customs, and different smells.[1] That's certainly true for any adult immersing themselves in the world of toddlers or adolescents.

---

1 There's a good chance Zacchaeus spoke with Jesus in a language that wasn't Jesus' native first language. Due to changes of power in the Roman province of Palestine, it was common for the people to speak Aramaic, Hebrew, Greek, and Latin.

Jesus demonstrated what it looks like to comfortably step into someone else's world. When you are comfortable in someone else's context, you send a powerful message of acceptance.

You can't force your way into someone's heart, but you can invite yourself into someone's world. When you immerse yourself in a kid's context, you answer underlying questions like . . .
Do you understand my everyday world?
Do you understand what shapes my perspective?
Do you understand why I do what I do?

If you are leading a group of kids or teenagers and find yourself thinking, "I can't understand why anyone would . . ." that should be a cautionary flag. The shallow response is to view this thought as a badge of moral superiority. "I'm so elevated in my thinking I really cannot fathom their mindset or behavior." But what if we responded to that thought in a personal way? What if, instead, we viewed it as a confession of our own limited perspective? "I can't understand why anyone would . . . so I need to take steps to learn more about their context."

SOMETHING CHANGES IN A RELATIONSHIP WHEN YOU TAKE THE TIME TO UNDERSTAND SOMEONE'S EVERYDAY CONTEXT.

It may seem presumptuous to invite yourself into someone's everyday life. What worked for Jesus probably doesn't work for you. You will need more than a one-liner before you show up at someone's house with twelve of your closest friends expecting dinner. But you may be surprised at how most people will welcome you into their community when you take the time to enter with sensitivity and respect.

WHEN YOU ENTER SOMEONE'S WORLD,
RESPECT THEIR PERSONALITY.
Everyone is unique. Some kids are more introverted; others are more extroverted. One kid may sit on your lap, whisper in your ear, and allow virtually zero personal space. Another kid may sit apart

from the group, bristle if you touch their shoulder, and feel safest when there's a healthy bubble between them and another person. Be intentional about learning each kid's unique needs and act accordingly.

WHEN YOU ENTER SOMEONE'S WORLD, RESPECT THEIR TIMELINE.

The road from shallow to personal may take months or even years. And you will enter a kid's world differently at different phases of their life. Preschoolers and kids who are elementary age tend to trust adults quickly. Young kids are likely to give you a report on the first day about someone they don't like, how much their mom weighs, or how your breath smells. Teenagers are frequently more guarded. That's one reason we encourage leaders to stay connected to a teenager for multiple years. It may take showing up consistently for 12 to 24 months before a teenager invites you into their personal world.

WHEN YOU ENTER SOMEONE'S WORLD, RESPECT THEIR BOUNDARIES.

Don't confuse being more personal with being too invasive. And make sure you work with parents, guardians, and organizational leadership to establish appropriate guardrails when you are inviting yourself into the lives of kids or teenagers. It's not just important for their safety, but for yours. Even if you're building a relationship with kids or teenagers outside the context of an official organization, it's smart to establish practical boundaries like staying public, doing things in a group, and keeping other adults informed.

Remember, you are moving from shallow to personal one step at a time. There is no clear formula for every relationship because we are all individuals. But by simply learning how to invite yourself into someone's life, you are becoming familiar with their context in a way that will help you understand their perspective. If you want to understand someone's perspective, here are five specific aspects of their world with which you should become familiar.

UNDERSTAND WHERE SOMEONE LIVES PHYSICALLY

A few years ago, we (Kristen and Reggie) initiated a project to help adults build empathy for the phases of a kid's life from birth through eighteen. We called it *The Phase Project*, and in its inaugural year we had an opportunity to create a video to help leaders experience what these first 936 weeks of life are like. For the video, we recreated a typical bedroom and simply rotated the furniture, bedding, clothing, and props as a way to illustrate the contextual changes in a kid's home environment.[2] We believed that visualizing the physical environment where a kid sleeps at night would help adults empathize with one of the most personal aspects of their world.

If you want to be personal it will help if you know something about the neighborhood, school, and physical home environment where a kid spends the majority of his or her time. Research in the education field shows how in-home visits impact parent participation and student learning. If you hope to influence a kid's spiritual growth, you may need to spend time at their school, in their community, or even in their house.

UNDERSTAND WHERE SOMEONE LIVES SOCIALLY

Just knowing about a person from their point of view can be shallow. We already mentioned the importance of knowing who a kid knows because it's one of their primary interests. But it's also important to know the people in a kid's world because they probably know something about that kid you would never know otherwise. When you know the people who know a person, you begin to see dimensions of a person you might have otherwise missed.

So, meet a kid's best friend, neighbor, cousin, sibling, or whoever is in their peer group. Meet a kid's teacher, coach, aunt or uncle, friend's parent, or whoever the significant adults are in their life. And meet a kid's primary caregiver.

The more you understand about a kid's social world, the easier it will be for you to become personal. In many cases, kids and

---

2 Search for "It's Just A Phase So Don't Miss It" on YouTube

teenagers need an advocate to help celebrate the distinctives of their family. They need someone who will hear conversations through their filter, considering the issues that are personal to them in a unique way because of the people they know.

UNDERSTAND WHERE SOMEONE LIVES DIGITALLY

One of the best illustrations of entering another person's digital space may be the 2018 film *Eighth Grade*. Movie producers intermix the face-to-face, personal encounters of an eighth-grade girl's home and school life with the digital content she produces for her vlog and the digital content she consumes through social networks.

Sure, when you follow someone online, you will see a filtered version of that person's life. But you may also see aspects of a person they may not feel comfortable sharing face-to-face. In a generation where digital spaces are increasingly more a part of our daily lives, it's difficult to be personal with someone without following the content they share about themselves online.

If you really want to understand another person's perspective, you probably need to listen to a few of the voices they listen to. It's easier than ever to place ourselves in a digital echo chamber where only our own opinions are repeated back to us. Think about it. You decide whether you watch Fox News or CNN. You decide whether you follow Jim Nantz or Alessia Cara. You scroll a social media feed filled only with the opinions of people who are your digital friends, and if you disagree with too many of their posts, you can unfollow. If you want to be personal, you may need to intentionally listen to conversations you wouldn't otherwise be part of.

UNDERSTAND WHERE SOMEONE LIVES CULTURALLY

All of my (Kristen's) extended family are from West Texas. I'm not sure if it's a Texas thing or just my family, but when you come to my house you can wear your muddy boots everywhere except in the bed (maybe). One of my best friends in high school was a first-generation U.S. citizen whose parents grew up in China. I learned very quickly that in most Asian homes, you are expected to remove your shoes at the door and walk through the house barefoot.

If you're from Boston and you visit a small town in the South, most people will smile and wave at you. It's every extrovert's dream. What you may not know, however, is that Southerners will wave at you even if they don't like you. If you go to Boston, people don't wave or smile no matter what they think of you.

When you are personal, you learn interesting nuances about a person's family and cultural practices. Knowing what a family does before mealtime, how a family celebrates holidays, and what acceptable topics of conversation are during a family gathering keeps you from staying shallow and making assumptions.

UNDERSTAND WHERE SOMEONE LIVES EMOTIONALLY

In the next chapter we will do a deep dive into what it means to examine our emotional lives. But you can't understand a kid's context without paying attention to some of the emotions that surround them on a daily basis.

Does a kid live in a loud home where adults fight, laugh, drink, or joke with each other openly? Does a kid live in a quiet home where adults seldom express anything openly? Are there things in a kid's environment that evoke fear, stress, shame, pride, or anger?

The key to developing empathy is not having lived the same experience as someone else, but tapping into the same emotion someone else is feeling and feeling it with them.

NEVER ASSUME YOU KNOW HOW SOMEONE FEELS,
UNTIL YOU HAVE TAKEN THE TIME TO SEE HOW THEY LIVE.

NEVER ASSUME YOU KNOW HOW SOMEONE FEELS,
UNTIL YOU HAVE INTERACTED WITH THE PEOPLE IN THEIR LIFE.

NEVER ASSUME YOU KNOW HOW SOMEONE FEELS,
UNTIL YOU HAVE ACTUALLY INQUIRED HOW THEY FEEL.

This world would change if more of us would stop assuming and start interacting. That's what it means to be personal. It's hard to be shallow when you know someone's name, know someone's interests, and know where someone lives. (When you get close enough to someone else, you won't want to go back to shallow living.)

That's how Jesus lived. And it changed the people He met. Zacchaeus left home alone and returned home with Jesus. Imagine what could change if the average kid was really convinced that Jesus wanted to go home with them.

What would it change if they actually believed they would never walk into any everyday situation alone ever again?

What would it change if the same Jesus in Zacchaeus' story went home with them? Could it change their future?

You're probably thinking, "That's a great idea. But that's impossible." Maybe not. Since you have Jesus in you. Why don't you just do it?

BE PERSONAL ENOUGH TO DO WHAT JESUS DID.
KNOW THEIR NAME.
STOP TO REALLY SEE THEM.
DISCOVER THEIR DAILY CONTEXT.

You may never convince a kid that Jesus cares about them, if you don't get personal. It probably feels impossible to be that personal with everyone. So don't. Just do it for a few. Ignore the crowd. Start with one. That's what Jesus did.

DO YOU KNOW WHERE I LIVE?

WHEN YOU KNOW WHERE I LIVE YOU MODEL EMPATHY, SO I HAVE HOPE THAT I AM WORTH KNOWING.

Take the time to understand someone's everyday context

IT'S PERSONAL

CHAPTER 5

DO YOU KNOW
WHAT I HAVE DONE?

I (Virginia) often get calls in the middle of the night from young people who are afraid to call their parents. Prior to my parenting years, I made an agreement with our youth that they could call at any time for a "rescue" with minimal questions. The only requirement was that they would have to go straight home.

One night Tony called for a ride home in the wee hours of the morning with the explanation that he was somewhere he was not supposed to be. My husband and I picked him up and took him to his mother's house. On the drive, our car became a confessional booth for his current and past sins. Prior to getting out of the car he asked, "Do you still love me?" We reassured Tony that our love for him was real, and then he entered his house to face the music with his mother.

You might lead a hundred kids and only need this chapter for one. The majority of the kids you lead may never call you at 2 a.m. or make a vulnerable confession to you. They shouldn't. You can't responsibly carry every kid's full disclosure. And most of what we talk about in this chapter won't happen in a group setting during regularly scheduled programming. It shouldn't. There are some pretty dark things that happen in a kid's physical or emotional world that don't need to be discussed in a group.

NO ONE NEEDS TO BE KNOWN BY EVERYONE,
BUT EVERYONE NEEDS SOMEONE WHO KNOWS THEM.

When you show up consistently over time to know a kid's name, interests, and context, you become personal. And when you are personal in this way, you cultivate trust. Trust is both powerful and fragile. One of the most devastating things you can do is to behave as if you are personal right up to the moment a kid trusts you with something they have done, only to respond in a shallow way.

Before we go any further, we probably need to clarify something.

The reason my husband and I picked up Tony wasn't to assuage his guilt and help him feel okay about his choices. On the contrary, I think the simple reality of seeing our faces that night made his guilt even more palpable. He had to make the phone call. He had to walk to our car knowing we knew where he was. He had to ride in a car with us all the way home knowing the price of his ride was full disclosure to his mother about where he had been (a much higher price than an Uber ride). *We didn't need to say a word to reinforce his guilt.*

When we showed up that night, we didn't alleviate Tony's guilt, but we did short-circuit what might have become a destructive shame narrative. We did not allow his internal monologue to progress from "Look what I did" to "Look at the person I've become. No one could ever love me."

Jesus demonstrated this same response when he stopped to invite himself to Zacchaeus' house for a meal. Have you ever considered how wildly offensive it was for Jesus to eat dinner with Zacchaeus?

First, Zacchaeus' position in Jericho was upheld through extortion. He wasn't a thief. He was much worse than a thief because his embezzlement was supported, rather than condemned, by those in power. He was the epitome of a corrupt leader who leverages the system for personal gain.

Second, many were coming to regard Jesus as the Messiah, the promised one. Just as leaders in the church are often regarded as personifications of the Church's interests, Jesus' actions might be seen as representations of the coming Kingdom. So for Him to share a meal with Zacchaeus was tantamount to inviting the tax tyrant to the messianic banquet and eternal blessings.[1]

Consider how this encounter might have felt to someone close to Jesus. Imagine you were Judas Iscariot experiencing this second-to-final week of Jesus' ministry.

Nothing seemed to make sense anymore. One minute Jesus was preaching about the Kingdom of Heaven and Judas felt certain they were on their way into Jerusalem to overthrow Pilate and dispose of Caiaphas. The next minute Jesus seemed to be predicting His own death. Jesus delayed a visit to his friend Lazarus' home for so long Lazarus died. Then Judas watched, along with countless others, as Jesus brought Lazarus out of his tomb fully alive three days after his burial. But none of these events may have seemed as strange as the encounter on the road to Jericho.

As they entered the city, Jesus paused to call a grown man down from a tree beside the road. When the man descended the tree Judas recognized signs of the man's profession at once. This was a tax collector. And from the looks of him, this wasn't just any tax collector. Jericho was a wealthy city, but this man appeared to have wealth even beyond what was typical for his trade.

Judas followed in silence as this man, Zacchaeus, led Jesus and the rest of their group into the atrium of the largest home he'd ever been inside. The ornate marble columns and elaborate

---

1 For a discussion of this messianic banquet: N.T. Wright, Jesus and the Victory of God (Minneapolis: Fortress Press, 1996), 431

mosaic floor were of a size and grandeur Judas associated with a country villa rather than an average city domicile. Extravagance was everywhere. It made Judas' stomach clench just to see it. This wealth could never have been acquired by fair taxation.

Judas took in the arrested expression on the faces of the servants. From the look of it, they weren't accustomed to receiving guests. Well, that at least made sense. Zacchaeus couldn't be well-liked in the community.

Fascinated, Judas watched as Zacchaeus ordered their meal as though their arrival was a well-planned event. "Boiled eggs, cheese, bread, and honey," Zacchaeus said excitedly. "Then bring out the fish and the oysters." Here Zacchaeus actually caught Judas's eyes. "Yes, all the oysters you can find!" he elaborated.

The party made their way across to the dining area and Judas' eyes widened yet again at the table already set with apples, pears, figs, pomegranates, cherries, and apricots. He couldn't remember ever seeing such a display of fruits.

As everyone took their places around the table, Judas watched Jesus carefully. Hadn't He commanded a man of similar wealth to give every single possession to the poor? Surely Jesus was preparing a similar mandate for this man Zacchaeus?

But Jesus seemed to be thoroughly enjoying His meal as though He were blissfully unaware of the financial crimes that must have paid for this feast. What's more, Jesus seemed unconcerned with the conversations happening around them as they ate. How was Jesus going to justify this indulgence? How could it possibly be acceptable to share a banquet of this magnitude with this sinner? No, more than a sinner. *A chief tax collector.*

Jesus seemed interested only in Zacchaeus. It was as if He could see past the luxury that was in such stark contrast to their typical wilderness wanderings and had eyes only for the man He had called out of a tree. With every bite, Jesus seemed to be saying, "Yes, Zacchaeus, I love you enough to share this meal with you."

And with every drink of wine, Jesus seemed to suggest, "You are not as alone as you think, Zacchaeus. There's a place for you at My table, too."

WHEN JESUS ATE WITH ZACCHAEUS JESUS MODELED **LOVE**.

It's interesting that Zacchaeus repents, even though Jesus never speaks about Zacchaeus' sin. In fact, in this part of the story Jesus doesn't really *do* anything. There is no moment when Jesus walks through the home inquiring how Zacchaeus bought this statue or asks whether the food on their plates was justly acquired. He does not declare, "I will sit with you for dinner once you repay the people as Jewish law requires."

Maybe that's because Jesus knew "should" and "must" are extrinsic, shallow motives for change. **When a person makes changes to their life as a way to please someone, perform for someone, or perfect their image, those changes are often short-lived.**

Kids and teenagers will make choices they shouldn't.
And, once a caring adult has communicated moral or behavioral expectations, kids and teenagers typically feel guilty about their wrong behaviors. *(Kids and teenagers are people. And guilt is kind of inherent to the human condition).*

For young people, guilt might sound like . . .
I spilled my drink.
I put my shirt on backward.
I forgot my homework.
I said really mean things to my friend.
I looked for pornography online.
I think I might have an addiction to pills.

Kids often feel real and meaningful guilt that can intrinsically motivate changes for their future. Such as, *"Next time, I will be more careful around my drink."* Or, *"In the future, I will write down my homework assignments in my agenda."*

Sometimes, though, kids and teenagers don't express their guilt in a way that feels sufficient to an adult. So one of the shallow responses adults often use with young people is to "yes, and" their guilt until it becomes a deeper sense of shame.

These adult responses often come from a place of fear. *If you don't know how bad you are, then you might never turn this thing around.*

Author and speaker Brené Brown defines shame as "the intensely painful feeling or experience of believing that we are flawed and therefore unworthy of love and belonging."[2] If guilt is a person's awareness that they have done something bad, shame is the belief that they *are* bad.

To elaborate on the examples above,
shame might sound like . . .
I spilled my drink because I'm a clumsy person who never does anything right.
I forgot my homework because I'm stupid and will never measure up to expectations.
I looked at pornography because I'm a dirty person who does unspeakable things and no one could ever love me.

The greatest trick shame plays on us is its ability to alienate us from the one thing that might help—love. When a person feels unlovable, they often begin to act in ways that make them harder to love. In the absence of love, shame has full permission to run rampant through our conscious and unconscious mind.

There are also scenarios where a kid or teenager may feel shame not because of what they have done, but from what has been done to them directly or indirectly.

In these instances their shame narrative may sound something like . . .

I am ugly because families like mine are ugly.

---

2 Brené Brown, *Daring Greatly: How the Courage to Be Vulnerable Transforms the Way We Live, Love, Parent and Lead* (New York: Avery, an Imprint of Penguin Random House, 2012), 69

I get hit because I'm a bad person who deserves it.
I exist to please others and don't have the right to decide who
touches me.

"Do you know what I've done?" and "Do you know what's been done to me?" are often closely related in kids. For them, the line may feel blurry. Kids are quick to assume that violence done to them by adults, or by peers, is somehow their fault and deserved. It's uncomfortable to hear the lies young people might tell themselves. There's obviously a difference between spilling a drink and being the victim of systemic abuse. However, regardless of what initiates or perpetuates a kid's shame narrative, it is always destructive.

When shame shuts down a young person's self-worth, it prevents them from moving forward. What's more, shame is often cyclical. People who feel intense shame are often likely to impose shame on those who have less power than themselves.

Jesus came to break this cycle. That's the power of the Gospel, and the power of Jesus' encounter with Zacchaeus. Jesus didn't enter Zacchaeus' house to impose shame upon Zacchaeus so he would accept Jesus as Messiah. Jesus entered Zacchaeus' house to demonstrate His love for Zacchaeus, and to rescue him from a cycle of shame that Zacchaeus could not break on his own.

Whenever a kid or teenager entrusts you with information about their world, you have an opportunity to break the power of shame.

WHEN YOU DEMONSTRATE LOVE IN THE FACE OF
SOMEONE'S DEEPEST VULNERABILITY, YOU ANSWER
A NUMBER OF UNSPOKEN QUESTIONS LIKE . . .
DO YOU THINK I WILL BE OKAY?
DO YOU THINK I STILL HAVE VALUE?
DO YOU THINK I CAN BE FORGIVEN?

As church leaders, we are often quick to teach kids, "God loves you." But many kids have a hard time knowing what love feels like unless they have experienced the love of a caring adult. We say,

"Jesus forgives you." But when shame has a stronghold on a young person's life, they are likely to think, "You're only saying that because you don't know me, and you don't know what I have done."

YOU DEMONSTRATE FORGIVENESS WHEN YOU LEARN TO RESPOND TO SOMEONE IN A WAY THAT REPLACES SHAME WITH HOPE.

When you see a kid's source of shame and respond with love, you prove they are worth loving. And when a kid rejects their shame narrative and believes they are worth the love you demonstrate, they will discover a new kind of hope. It's the hope that inspired Zacchaeus to return four times what he had stolen. It's the kind of hope that says, "Your past does not define your future." It's the hope that comes when you realize the power of the Gospel.

At this point, you may be thinking, "Okay. But surely I can't just eat at a kid's house one time and heal centuries of generational shame." You're right. You aren't Jesus, and this will take longer than one afternoon *cena*. Here are a few practical techniques we've learned through experience and by listening to other wise leaders who work with kids and teenagers.

EXAMINE YOUR MOTIVE FOR INVOLVEMENT

You don't need to examine your motive before you learn a person's name. However, you may want to examine your calendar to make sure you have time to consistently show up before you discover too much about a kid's interests or context. And, when it comes to the deeper and most vulnerable parts of a kid or teenager's story, you cannot simply walk in uninvited.

Jesus was Jesus.
You are not.

You are not responsible to know the answer to this question for every kid you know. But you are responsible for how you respond to those kids who trust you with their story.

When a kid trusts you with something they have done, you will naturally want to help them move in a better direction. You will want to fix their behavior. Before you formulate your lecture, pause and ask yourself this question: Do I want this kid to change their behavior because I believe it's the right thing to do? Or do I want this kid to change their behavior because I love her?

In ministry settings, we often use the term accountability as an excuse for shallow discipleship. Accountability gone wrong almost always sounds like, "Stop doing that. It's wrong. I can tell it's wrong. Everyone who knows you can tell it's wrong. Why don't you see that it's wrong?" Accountability in a more personal, and far more authentic sense sounds more like, "Stop doing this. It's killing you. You're miserable. You're not yourself. This isn't about what's right or wrong. I'm standing by you until we can get you out of this."

There may be times when you are not qualified to help a kid with the story they entrust to you. If you are personal, you are likely to find yourself in the middle of some stories that are well above your pay grade. In the book *Lead Small*, we encourage volunteers to talk with their leader whenever a kid shares one of what we call "the three hurts."

When a kid is being hurt.
When a kid is hurting others.
When a kid is hurting himself.

These are times when getting help from another trusted adult, someone you know is qualified to handle the situation, is the best way to be personal.

NOTICE PATTERNS OR CHANGES IN A KID'S BEHAVIOR
Sometimes you won't know what kind of shame a kid is carrying. Okay, most of the time you won't.

In chapter three, we mentioned the importance of knowing a kid's interests so you can recognize when a kid is up a tree. Practically speaking, the more you know about a kid, the more you will pick up on changes in behavior that may indicate when a kid is caught in a negative shame cycle.

Some kids may love to tell shocking stories simply for the thrill of a good reaction. This isn't vulnerability and it probably isn't exposing the real reason for their shame. Some kids may act aggressively as a way to bring order to their emotional world by proving to themselves the validity of their shame narrative. *"See, I knew no one would love me."* Some kids may withdraw from people in an act of self-preservation. Some, often the most difficult to see, simply respond to debilitating and corrosive shame by being very, very good kids.

When you make the choice to be personal in a kid's world, you begin to realize that every behavior has a purpose. Observing those behaviors may help you recognize when a kid needs help. Those same behaviors may also be an essential filter for your response if a kid shares something personal with you.

INVOLVE PARENTS WHENEVER POSSIBLE

One of the fastest and most effective ways to understand the "why" behind a kid's behavior is to convene the adults who know the kid best. Volunteers, mentors, teachers, and coaches are often quick to raise a flag when something is happening in a kid's world. But most of the time, parents are even quicker to know why it's happening.

Before becoming parents, all three of us were limited in our ability to understand just how delicate this kind of conversation with a parent really is. Because a parent knows their kid's pattern so much better than we do as leaders, they often feel the weight of a kid's situation more intensely. Family relationships are intricately connected, and kids who are hurting often live with parents who are hurting. So it's challenging for any parent to hear from someone outside their home their kid is working through guilt and shame, without the parents themselves feeling accused.

When you notice changes in a kid's behavior and wish to consult a parent, begin with the assumption you might be wrong about your interpretation. Say things like, "I'm curious . . ." or "I have noticed . . . and I was wondering if you have noticed as well."

When you hear a kid's confession and decide to bring a parent into the conversation, help a parent save face. It's normal for kids and teenagers to confess to adults who are not their parents, but it's often hard for a parent to understand why. Help a confused and afraid parent interpret the conversation with reassuring statements like, "Your son told me something I know he would want you to know." Or, "Your daughter so highly values your opinion of her that it's extremely hard for her to share this with you."

Regardless of a parent's initial response, it's worth it to continually advocate for the healthiest parent-child relationship possible. Pray for the entire family. And find professional help whenever necessary.

NAME WHAT NEEDS NAMING

In her book *Daring Greatly*, Brené Brown says, "Shame derives its power from being unspeakable. That's why it loves perfectionists— it's so easy to keep us quiet."

One of the fastest ways to cut shame off at the knees is to simply name what's happening out loud.

The younger a child is, the more quickly they might trust you with a seemingly vulnerable life event. The older a kid is, especially in the teenage years, the more deeply he or she might feel shame.

If you sense that a teenager needs to say something, it's always best to help them say it first. If you are in a physically and emotionally safe place, you might say something like, "Is there something you want me to know?" Or, "Are you holding onto something you don't know how to discuss with me?"

If a teenager is unlikely to name something, *and you have earned trust over time*, you might go first in the naming process. These moments are almost a kind of intervention and will require love in generous proportion.

Going first may sound like . . .

"I know you are pregnant. You haven't told anyone close to you and I'm wondering why."

"I know you haven't been eating enough food to be healthy for some time. Is this something we can talk about?"

"I know you sent a video to a lot of kids at school last week and it really hurt some people. Are you okay?"

REDEFINE WHAT NEEDS REDEFINED

Shame is a social construct that derives power from our natural fear of isolation. This is one of the core reasons that being personal is the antidote to shallow living. When you know that someone knows you, and knows what you've done, and they still show up at your house for dinner you might begin to have hope that you are forgivable.

Every person needs to know they are more than the sum of their worst moments. Whether it's decisions they have made or actions that were done to them, kids need someone to boldly remind them, "This isn't who you are." And, "This isn't who you have to become."

When a kid or teenager has suffered abuse or abandonment, they need someone to repeatedly remind them, "This is not your fault."

When a kid or a teenager has done something wrong, they need to know there is still good inside them and they can still be accepted and loved. God's image does not suddenly leave us the moment we sin.

Being guilty is part of being human.
But living with shame is something you choose.

Jesus came so we could all choose freedom. He died and rose again so we could fully live the way we were created to live.[3]

---

3 John 10:10

EMPATHIZE PERSONALLY AND PUBLICLY

When someone shares something confessional, it's natural to compare the experience they describe with your own experience in order to look for common ground. But remember, empathy requires you to feel another person's emotion. It doesn't require you to have lived another person's experience.

There is a danger in responding to a kid's story by overly sharing your own story. While telling your own story may feel as if it makes the situation relatable, if you aren't careful, you hijack their moment of vulnerability and make it about yourself

Your story may also blind you to some of the ways a kid or teenager's experience differs from your own. Learn to listen to their story without superimposing your own history. Instead, practice empathy.

Educator and author Catherine Stonehouse says, "Children are most like adults in their feelings."[4] That means while differences in stature and maturity may be obvious, when it comes to emotions, we can relate to kids more than we think.
Try leveraging your experience to tap into the familiar emotion as you listen.

We have said repeatedly that deeply confessional and vulnerable moments are best in one-on-one settings. But nothing will determine whether a kid trusts you with a personal confession more than the way you communicate publicly.

Kids are smart. They are listening to the way you . . .
talk about people in the news.
share stories about your friends and family.
talk about (or hopefully don't talk about) other kids or teenagers.

If they sense that you are quick to judge, easy to alarm, or prone to gossip, you can be almost certain they will not trust you with something confessional. (They probably shouldn't).

---

4 Catherine Stonehouse, Joining Children on the Spiritual Journey: Nurturing a Life of Faith (Grand Rapids: Baker Academic, 1998), 70

One of the reasons Jesus' encounter with Zacchaeus was so powerful is because of what it communicated to those who were watching.

Imagine one more time that you were sitting at the table in Jericho. Maybe you see Judas looking across the table at his friends Peter, James, and John who are deep in a conversation of their own. Maybe Thomas is laughing at something Bartholomew just said. Then, you notice Matthew. Consider Matthew, the former tax collector turned disciple, sitting slightly apart from the rest with an uncomfortable look on his face.

The way Jesus treated Zacchaeus must have felt personal to Matthew. If Matthew ever doubted whether he was fully forgiven, Jesus' forgiveness of Zacchaeus must have been a confirmation of hope.

In the same way, how you respond to a kid or teenager's confession may give hope to more than one. There are kids and teenagers all around us who need someone to answer the question, "Do you know what I've done?" in a way that gives them hope for the future.

DO YOU KNOW WHAT I HAVE DONE?

WHEN YOU KNOW WHAT I HAVE DONE YOU MODEL LOVE, SO I HAVE HOPE THAT I AM WORTH FORGIVING.

Respond to someone in a way that replaces shame with hope

IT'S PERSONAL

CHAPTER 6

DO YOU KNOW
WHAT I CAN DO?

I (Reggie) was average in school. One of the hardest years for me was ninth grade when my parents moved from Memphis, Tennessee, to Albany, Georgia, in the *middle of the school year*. I left everyone—friends, teachers, coaches, everyone—and started over just a few months before my 16th birthday. Maybe you can tell I'm still a little bitter.

I felt lost as I tried to navigate a new school, with no friends, where I was already behind in most of the classes. That's probably why the history class taught by Coach Carl Williams made such an impression on me.

Coach Williams' teaching style was a cross between a late-night host and a stand-up comedian. He always started class with an opening act (sometimes a song), and I distinctly remember the historic accounts of romance and intrigue he talked about. I'll never forget how he stopped me one day after class to ask if I would be willing to teach a series about the history of Hebrew culture. He handed me a teacher's book. Then he smiled and said, "Don't leave out the scandalous stuff."

I have always been an introvert. An alarm went off in my mind screaming, "No way! I am only sixteen years old. Why me?" It's hard to explain what happened that year, but it influenced the rest of my life.

I'm sure my presentation was not nearly as good as I remember it, but I do recall Coach Williams cheering me on during the entire process. I owe him for believing I could do something I had no idea I could do.

I (Kristen) don't like to talk much about my middle school years. I've always been petite in size, so just picture a 13-year-old who doesn't look a day over nine in the heart of the grunge era (baggy jeans and oversized flannel shirts).

In addition to my above-average awkwardness, my parents separated the day after Christmas when I was in seventh grade and finalized their divorce in April of my eighth-grade year. During those years, my GPA dropped drastically, and I lost all sense of direction.

Most adults weren't sure what to do with me. My teachers were frustrated by my lack of effort. My parents weren't sure how to handle my absolutely delightful attitude. (I ran away from home twice during that time frame—mature, I know). But one teacher saw what even I had failed to see.

Catherine Burroughs sat down with me in the library of Peachtree Junior High, pointed to a failed assignment I'd turned in, and said, "This isn't who you are." She was the first person to tell me that my changed attitude and academic direction weren't me. She said she didn't know what was happening in my life, but she suspected I was hurting.

She told me not to worry about fixing my grades before I took the time to fix me.

Then she did something sneaky. She called the teacher who sponsored the high school yearbook and told her to look for me because I was good with words. Four years later, I was the editor-in-chief for the Dunwoody High School *Chrysalis* yearbook.

I (Virginia) have always been the "odd person" in any group. I didn't feel like I fit in at school, at church, or even in my family at times. As an African American girl growing up in the 1960s, my tendency to make myself heard wasn't always seen as a positive quality. Most adults still carried the attitude their parents passed to them, that "children should be seen and not heard."

Then when I was fifteen, Opal Adams became an adult leader in the youth department at my church.

She didn't see an odd, chatty, self-asserting teenager.
She saw a confident, articulate leader.

Something in the way she saw me changed the way I saw myself. She said I could help run the youth ministry, and she made me vice president of what we called *YPD*, the Young People's Department.

When Opal Adams called me a leader, I began to think of myself as a leader for the first time. When I realized people wanted to hear what I could say, I began to work on improving my communication abilities rather than suppressing them. Suddenly, I felt like I could make a difference.

HERE'S THE POINT.
A LOT OF PEOPLE, ESPECIALLY KIDS AND TEENAGERS, NEED SOMEONE TO BELIEVE THEY CAN DO SOMETHING THEY MAY NOT EVEN REALIZE THEY CAN DO.

Actually, we could easily make the case that many of the people who believe in Jesus first believed because He saw their potential to live life at another level.

This seems obvious in the story of Zacchaeus. Let's go back one last time. You already know how it ends, but imagine again how Zacchaeus might have felt on that day when Jesus and His disciples sat enjoying a meal in his home. An uncomfortable emotion stirred in Zacchaeus as he looked around the table.

For years, Zacchaeus had spent every day building and furnishing this home.

He could remember every purchase he had ever made, and he knew the lengths to which he had gone to pay for it.

He knew his favorite merchants by name, and took every opportunity to fill his home with the newest fabric or the latest style.

He had obsessed about every plant in the garden, shopped for weeks for just the right marble to line the *impluvium*, and hired only the very best artisan to design the mosaic floor of the atrium.

But until this afternoon he had never realized how empty his home really was. He had never had friends around this table, and it made him feel very curious. *"What is it?"* he asked himself. *"How can this group of men somehow make my prized stone sculptures feel empty and cold?"*

THIS MORNING,
ZACCHAEUS HAD LEFT HOME ALONE.

THIS AFTERNOON,
ZACCHAEUS RETURNED HOME WITH FRIENDS.

THIS MORNING,
ZACCHAEUS WENT OUT TO SEE THE GREAT TEACHER.

THIS AFTERNOON,
ZACCHAEUS FELT AS IF HIS ENTIRE LIFE WAS CHANGING.

The sensation pushed and pulled at Zacchaeus until he could no longer stay silent. What was it he needed to do? *"Should I sing a song of gratitude?"* he thought in desperation. *"No. I've never been much of a singer."* He couldn't let this dinner end without somehow putting into words what this meal meant to him. It was changing him.

"When these men leave, I will never be able to return to my life as it was before," Zacchaeus thought. And suddenly he knew exactly what he needed to say.

Zacchaeus stood up and shouted without hesitation, "Here and now I give half of my possessions to the poor, and if I have cheated anybody out of anything I will pay back four times the amount." Relief and energy simultaneously flooded his body in a way he had never known before, and he knew this dinner wasn't the end of his quest for meaning. It was the start of a new life.

The servants and disciples were looking at Zacchaeus with surprise, but Jesus looked as though He knew every thought coursing through Zacchaeus' mind.

Jesus said, "Today salvation has come to this house, because this man, too, is a son of Abraham. For the Son of Man came to seek and to save the lost."

The story of Zacchaeus is a story of transformation. When some of us read terms like "salvation" and "lost," our minds quickly shift to ideas of eternity. Some might assume this is a great story about a man who decided to believe in Jesus so he could avoid spending eternity in Dante's Inferno. Be saved. Avoid Hell. But there's just so much more to this story.

When Jesus said, "Today, salvation has come to your house. Jesus was not simply saying, "You were going to Hell, but now you're going to Heaven."

Actually, it was more like Jesus was saying, "You were living in Hell, now you can start discovering what Heaven is like."

That's the power of the Gospel. It should never be limited to what happens after someone dies. The Gospel should always be thought of in the context of how it impacts someone's life while they are living.

WHEN JESUS SAID, "SALVATION HAS COME TO THIS HOUSE," JESUS MODELED BELIEF.

Okay. Yes, we know Zacchaeus wasn't saved *because* Jesus believed in Zacchaeus. It's the other way around. Maybe, like so many of us, Zacchaeus believed in Jesus because Jesus first believed in him.

Prior to meeting Jesus, Zacchaeus had lost his true sense of identity, belonging, and purpose. It wasn't intentional on his part. (It happens to the rest of us more than we admit.)

He lost his way because of his obsession with money, power, and position.

He forfeited relationships and created ongoing tensions with friends and family.

Chances are, he was a lonely man no one could trust. Worst of all, he was trapped in a corrupt government system and couldn't imagine a way out.

THEN JESUS SHOWED UP.

When Zacchaeus realized how Jesus saw him, everything changed. He realized his potential to be part of a remarkable story. He discovered he could give back to a community.

He dared to believe he could transform from a greedy tax collector into a generous friend.

Many of us get stuck for similar reasons. We aren't saying your career choice is the equivalent of a Roman publican. But, to oversimplify, Zacchaeus was up a tree for three reasons: greed, shame, and corruption. It's not too much of a stretch to say these three things represent the typical reasons people get disillusioned and discouraged with life.

THE TRAP OF SELF-DESTRUCTIVE HABITS

The path to self-destructive habits is always subtle. It starts with one experience that makes you feel good. That experience leads to another, and another, and another, until whatever the habit is, it no longer brings you pleasure.

If you've ever struggled with addiction, or known someone who struggled with addiction, you know how debilitating this can be. It doesn't matter if it's alcohol, opioids, spending, sex, lying, purging, or cutting. It's always a trap. And it's almost impossible to get unstuck on your own.

THE TRAP OF UNRESOLVED EMOTIONS

We all have emotions. Some feel more than others. But having emotions is not the problem. Not knowing how to respond to emotions can become a psychological trap.

If you've ever found yourself in a negative mental spiral through jealousy, unforgiveness, anger, or shame, you probably know how exhausting it can be. It can lead to a decline in physical health. It can sabotage your ability to give and receive love or to connect with others in a meaningful way.

THE TRAP OF OVERWHELMING CIRCUMSTANCES

Life is hard, and we all struggle. But we don't all struggle the same way. In chapter four, we encouraged you to learn more about where someone lives. It's hard to measure the generational impact of poverty, illiteracy, displacement, unemployment, or incarceration. Systemic issues in a community often contribute to despair.

People (even kids and teenagers) can get caught in a system and not know how to break free. Actually, we could argue that Zacchaeus was caught in a system of privilege—upholding the system while being hurt by the system, and hurting others through the system.

Zacchaeus was trapped by habits, emotions, and circumstances. So if there's hope for Zacchaeus, then maybe there's hope for anyone. Jesus modeled the idea that sometimes people need a tangible,

physical representation of God to simply remind them . . .
"You are good enough to be able to do good."
"You are loved enough to be able to love someone."
"You are forgiven enough to be able to change."

> **MAYBE YOU NEED TO BE PERSONAL ENOUGH TO BELIEVE IN SOMEONE'S POTENTIAL TO LIVE A REMARKABLE STORY.**

Coach Williams, Catherine Burroughs, and Opal Adams all understood the importance of believing in someone's potential. You probably know the name of one or two people who did the same for you.

But consider this. What these leaders did was much more than simply recognizing a skill set. We often think answering the question, "Do you know what I can do?," means identifying someone's talent. We think it sounds like . . .
"Wow, look at that picture you drew!"
"Good game, man."
"You're so smart."

In reality, these are fairly shallow affirmations.
When adults praise kids or teenagers for their achievement and success, they often send a subtle message, "You are good because you won this time."

The problem with shallow praise is that it constructs an identity that falls to pieces when challenged by failure, unmet expectations, or even a change in circumstances. The kid who grows up with an identity wrapped around his on-court game may hit a wall when he reaches the end of his basketball career.

Social and developmental psychologist Carol Dweck forever changed the way counselors and educators motivate a child based on what she calls "a growth mindset."[1] Decades of research now support her discovery that the human brain is malleable, and

---

1 To learn more about growth mindset, check out Carol Dweck on TED by searching "The Power of Believing that You Can Improve."

intelligence is not fixed. Here's what that means:

No kid is smart enough to avoid academic failure.
But all kids, regardless of their grades, can become smarter.

No kid is athletic enough to win every game.
But all kids, regardless of their coordination, can become stronger.

The way you speak to a person shapes the way that person's brain builds connections. So instead of praising their ability, it's far better to encourage a kid's effort. Instead of praising a kid's achievement, you would do better to praise a kid's character development.

The more personal you are, the more specific you can be with the encouragement you give.

Here's the point. If a kid or teenager is stuck due to systemic issues, emotional processing, or poor choices, they will need more than talent to help them move forward. They need adults who encourage their developing character so they will have the kind of integrity and grit needed in order to change.

I (Reggie) attended a symposium last year about poverty and disadvantaged kids. Someone on a panel made the point that most people who are born in poverty stay in poverty. They went on to observe that kids who break this cycle do so because of a sponsor, not because of a talent.

We think the same is true whether a kid is stuck in their emotional development or poor choices. Kids and teenagers need someone who believes in their potential to live remarkably.

Every kid needs someone to believe in their potential so they know they are worth helping.

**WHEN YOU BELIEVE IN A KID'S POTENTIAL,
YOU ANSWER A FEW UNDERLYING QUESTIONS LIKE . . .**
DO YOU BELIEVE IN MY DREAMS?
DO YOU BELIEVE I HAVE WHAT IT TAKES?
DO YOU BELIEVE I CAN DO SOMETHING MEANINGFUL?

The application for this chapter is pretty simple.

If you want to step in, show up, and be personal, a great place to start is by helping a kid believe they can do these three things: Help someone believe they can do good, that they can offer real love, and that they can change in ways that matter.

HELP SOMEONE BELIEVE, "I CAN DO GOOD"
Most of us are programmed to see the bad. Maybe you're reading this and you're already theologically uncomfortable because we haven't talked enough about just *how bad* people are. Aren't we all sinners who have fallen short of the glory of God?

I (Reggie) was constantly reminded of this thought when I was growing up. I can't reach God without Jesus. My sin placed me so far from God that I needed the cross to bridge the gap between God and myself. I still believe this is true.

But what no one ever really explained to me about Romans 3:23 is that if you and I "fall short of God's glory," it must mean we are already part of the way there. Have you ever considered the idea that humans are closer to the image of God than any other part of creation?[2]

What if we decided our job as leaders in the Church is to look for the spark in every kid or teenager?

Look for the image of God that already exists, and then become personal enough to earn the trust and credibility to say, "You are good enough to do something good."

Wouldn't this dramatically impact a kid's identity?

---

2 Hebrews 2:7-9, Psalm 8:4-6

Wouldn't it give them a foundation for the kind of faith that's strong enough to withstand any circumstances?

HELP SOMEONE BELIEVE, "I CAN LOVE SOMEONE"

On the surface, this may not seem relevant to helping a kid get unstuck. But God not only created humans in His image, God designed humans so they need other humans.

Relationships are central to God's design, which is why someone's potential is compromised whenever a person makes choices, battles emotions, or encounters systems that alienate them from healthy relationships.[3] They lose their sense of belonging.

This is the reason we spent so much time in the last chapter unpacking the importance of personally showing up in a kid's world to model forgiveness.

Whenever a kid or teenager allows shame to erode their self-worth, they minimize their view of God's great creation. They devalue Christ's sacrifice on their behalf. They limit their ability to receive love, or give love to others. That's shallow living.

One of our roles as leaders is to become personal enough to communicate, "You are loved enough to be able to love others."

HELP SOMEONE BELIEVE, "I CAN CHANGE"

Maybe the worse thing we can think or say about anyone is, "They will never change." It may sound like a reasonable presumption, unless you believe in Jesus. If you believe in Jesus, you probably also believe . . .

> everyone is created in God's image.
> Jesus came back to life.
> His Spirit is at work in believers.

Everything about our faith suggests anyone can change. That's why many philosophers and ethicists believe hope is a distinctively Christian virtue.

---

3 Genesis 2:18

When I (Kristen) was a senior in high school, I had a conversation with a friend who modeled what it sounds like to tell somebody, "You just cannot change."

I stood outside my dad's apartment with this friend discussing my future. "You should choose the Christian university," he insisted, "because your parents are divorced which means you have a shallow foundation for your morals. If you go to a state school, you're destined to make bad choices and lose your faith."

I don't know what this friend had been reading, or why he felt entitled to leverage my family's story against me. I don't actually care whether research supports his argument. All I cared about in the moment was how it stung to have someone believe I was trapped in some alternate reality because of my family history.

How many kids and teenagers need someone to believe they are able to break free?

Kids need someone to see they are
trapped by their own choices,
and convince them they are capable
of changing their behavior.

They need someone to see the
emotional battle raging inside,
and believe they can change the internal dialogue.

They need someone to see
the systems that hold them back,
and advocate with them to find a way out.

Until leaders can become personal enough to give hope, kids and teenagers may never realize their God-given potential.

Anybody can show up in a moment and simply say,
"You can do good."
"You can love someone."
"You can change."

But it will never have the same kind of impact as
when the message comes from . . .
SOMEONE WHO KNOWS YOU,
SOMEONE WHO KNOWS YOUR NAME,
SOMEONE WHO KNOWS WHAT MATTERS TO YOU,
SOMEONE WHO KNOWS WHERE YOU LIVE,
SOMEONE WHO KNOWS WHAT YOU HAVE DONE.

Affirmation and encouragement hold more weight when they
come from someone who has history with you. When a kid hears
these three statements from someone who really knows them,
they hear a silent and powerful *still* between the lines.

> "You can *still* do good."
> "You can *still* love someone."
> "You can *still* change."

There will be moments in everyone's life when they just need to
be reminded that they "still" can do what they can do. Your voice
could make the difference in someone's motivation to keep moving
in the right direction.

Throughout His ministry, Jesus seemed to give this kind of hope.
He knew people, and still believed they could do better than they
were doing.

He called Peter a rock.
He convinced His disciples they could change the world.

Then, when things went wrong, He told them again.

That's why you have a unique voice in kids' lives
when you know them personally.

They will need you to tell them what you have
already told them more than once.

They will need you to keep believing in them,
so they will keep believing in themselves.

THAT'S ACTUALLY WHAT HOPE IS.

Hope is knowing what someone can do,
and reminding them they can still do it.

Hope highlights someone's potential
to change the future regardless of the past.

Hope convinces someone to imagine
a better version of themselves.
It happens when someone gets personal enough to inspire
someone else to keep . . .
      Doing,
      Breathing,
      Creating,
      Giving,
      Loving,
      Growing,
      Believing, and
      Living a remarkable story.

EVERYBODY NEEDS SOMEBODY WHO KNOWS
THE ANSWER TO THE QUESTION,

DO YOU KNOW
WHAT I CAN DO?

WHEN YOU KNOW WHAT I CAN DO YOU MODEL BELIEF
SO I HAVE HOPE THAT I AM WORTH HELPING.

Believe in someone's potential
to live a remarkable story

IT'S PERSONAL

CHAPTER 7

START WITH SOMEONE

So, who are you in the Zacchaeus narrative?
Most of us take different roles simultaneously.

Sometimes we are in the crowd, watching as someone stops for the least likely person we would have imagined.

Occasionally, we will be tempted to whisper to a neighbor, "There's no point trying to help him."

Or, "Good luck with that one. She'll never change."

Or maybe you're not the whisperer,
but the neighbor who gives a sanctimonious nod in agreement.

DON'T BE FOOLED BY THE MAJORITY
If you had asked the crowd whose house Jesus should visit, Zacchaeus would have been their last choice. The majority isn't

always right. When someone stops to be personally involved in another person's story something remarkable can happen . . .
even when the person seems like a lost cause.
even when you disapprove of the person's life choices.
even when it's someone you've tried, and failed, to help before.

When you decide to live like it's personal, you see people in a different way. And you root for others who are stopping under sycamore trees.

Sometimes we are Zacchaeus, hiding behind the branches and looking for Jesus. Zacchaeus only climbed a tree once (that we know of). But, metaphorically speaking, you will probably climb a tree much more frequently.

One of the great Christian myths is that once you have
grown up,
accepted Jesus,
and become a leader,
you are completely over the need to climb a tree.

If you aren't careful, you will fall into the trap of thinking you exist only to be personal for someone, and forget that you also need someone to be personal for you.

ANYBODY HAS THE POTENTIAL TO GET STUCK

Kids, teenagers, volunteers, parents, mentors, pastors . . . we all get stuck. And when we do, we don't need a crowd of people. We need one person who is willing to stop and be personal enough to help us back down out of the tree and move us toward hope. It helps if you already know who that person might be, and you go ahead and voluntarily let them in on what's happening in your life long before you go hiding out in trees.

And sometimes you are Jesus. Actually, you are never Jesus. But for the sake of the illustration, sometimes you will be the one who will stop when someone else is stuck. It might not seem like a big deal to keep a short list of people you are personal for.

IT MAY SEEM SIMPLE TO . . .
KNOW SOMEONE'S NAME.
REMEMBER SOMEONE'S INTERESTS.
DISCOVER SOMEONE'S EVERYDAY CONTEXT.
BE SOMEONE WHO CAN BE TRUSTED
WITH SOMEONE'S CONFESSION.
HELP SOMEONE REALIZE WHAT HE OR SHE IS CAPABLE OF.

**BUT IT COULD HAVE A FAR
GREATER IMPACT THAN YOU CAN IMAGINE.**

IF YOU NEVER STOP, YOU'LL NEVER KNOW

What would have happened to Zacchaeus if Jesus hadn't stopped?
He might have stayed in the tree until the sun went down, and
then walked slowly home. Maybe he would have gone back to work
the next day, still collecting exorbitant taxes, still emotionally
empty and disillusioned with life.

That might not have seemed like a big deal to most of the people
in Jericho. They might have thought, "So what? Zacchaeus is
still Zacchaeus." But think about the difference—not only for
Zacchaeus, but for all the people who were influenced as a result of
Zacchaeus' life change.

**WHEN YOU STOP FOR ONE PERSON,
IT ALWAYS IMPACTS MORE THAN ONE.**

There's nothing wrong with gathering a large crowd, building a
large following, or gaining influence with a greater number of
people. Great leaders have accomplished incredible things from a
platform. But never underestimate the potential of what happens
when you get personal. On His way to the cross, Jesus went home
with one person. By being personal with one, He had an impact on
the entire city.

IT'S HARD TO BE PERSONAL IN A CROWD

When you started this book we promised the ideas here would
be the difference between being a fulfilled leader or a frustrated
volunteer. So, this is it:

If you want what you do to matter more,
you might need to become more personal for a few.

You can always be a little more personal with a lot of people.
But you can only ever be really personal with a few.

You might be able to remember the names of a few thousand
people if you really try.

You can probably remember one or two interests of a
hundred people.

You might visit the homes of a dozen people this year.

And if it gets personal, two or three kids might trust you enough
to tell you what they've done, and listen when you remind them of
what they are capable of doing.

You might just be someone's best chance to be seen.

Imagine there's someone around the next corner up a tree waiting
for you to show up. Until you see them, they will go on feeling
invisible and ignored. But starting today, that can change.
When you decide to be personal, they can start believing there's
hope. They can begin to embrace a new way of thinking. They can
be driven by a new internal monologue that says . . .

I AM NO LONGER INVISIBLE BECAUSE SOMEONE
KNOWS MY NAME.
I'M NOTICED. I'M MEMORABLE. I'M HONORED.

I AM NO LONGER INVISIBLE BECAUSE SOMEONE
KNOWS WHAT MATTERS TO ME.
I'M UNIQUE. I'M WORTHWHILE. I'M INTERESTING.

I AM NO LONGER INVISIBLE BECAUSE SOMEONE
KNOWS WHERE I LIVE.
I'M UNDERSTOOD. I'M ACCEPTED. I'M KNOWN.

I AM NO LONGER INVISIBLE BECAUSE SOMEONE KNOWS WHAT I HAVE DONE. I'M LOVED. I'M FORGIVEN. I'M HOPEFUL.

I AM NO LONGER INVISIBLE BECAUSE SOMEONE KNOWS WHAT I CAN DO. I'M SIGNIFICANT. I'M VALUABLE. I'M COURAGEOUS.

Zacchaeus is proof that when someone gets personal, it can change everything.

BIOS

VIRGINIA WARD

Virginia Ward serves as the Assistant Dean and Assistant Professor of Youth Ministry and Leadership at Gordon-Conwell Theological Seminary, Boston Campus, where she teaches classes in urban youth ministry and leadership. She makes ministry personal by inspiring, enlightening, and empowering individuals and organizations to equip the next generation of leaders.

Virginia's local and national involvement in the training and development of youth leaders spans three decades. She comes with extensive experience as an urban pastor, ministry organizer, and youth ministry expert. Virginia pursued education in ministry, earning a Master of Arts in Youth Ministry, and Doctor of Ministry in Emerging Generations at Gordon-Conwell Theological Seminary.

A third-generation minister, Virginia is an Associate Pastor at Abundant Life Church where her husband Lawrence Ward is the Senior Pastor and Bishop. They have two sons, Paul and Mark. Together they formed a consulting company, Wards of Wisdom to equip urban leaders and ministries seeking change.

Since 2014, Virginia has been a keynote speaker for Orange at its national conference in Atlanta and at Orange Tour venues across the nation. She's also serves with the DeVos Urban Leadership Initiative, and Intervarsity Christian Fellowship.

REGGIE JOINER

Reggie Joiner is founder and CEO of Orange/reThink Group, a nonprofit organization whose purpose is to influence those who influence the next generation. Orange provides resources and training for churches and organizations that create environments for parents, kids, and teenagers.

Before founding Orange in 2006, Reggie was one of the founders of North Point Community Church with Andy Stanley. During his 11 years there, Reggie was the executive director of family ministry.

Reggie has authored and co-authored several books including *Think Orange, A New Kind of Leader, Seven Practices of Effective Ministry, Parenting Beyond Your Capacity, Lead Small, Playing for Keeps, When Relationships Matter,* and *It's Just a Phase So Don't Miss It.*

Reggie and his wife, Debbie, live in North Georgia and have four adult children and four grandchildren.

For more information about Reggie Joiner, visit ReggieJoiner.com or follow him on Instagram @ReggieJoiner.

KRISTEN IVY

Kristen Ivy is executive director of messaging at Orange. She and her husband, Matt, have three young children and things can get very personal around their house.

Before beginning her career at reThink in 2006, Kristen earned her bachelors of education from Baylor University and a Master of Divinity from Mercer University. She worked in the public school system as a high school Biology and English teacher, where she learned firsthand the joy and importance of influencing the next generation.

At Orange, Kristen has played an integral role in the development of the elementary, middle school, high school, and parenting curriculums and has shared her experiences at speaking events across the country. Kristen is author of *It's Just a Phase So Don't Miss It*, *Playing for Keeps*, *When Relationships Matter,* and the 18-volume Phase Guides for parents.

For more information about Kristen Ivy,
visit KristenIvy.com or follow her on Instagram @_Kristen_Ivy.